Elementary School Evaluation:
Administrator's Guide to Accountability

Elementary School Evaluation: Administrator's Guide to Accountability

Eugene J. Bradford,
Albert F. Doremus,
and
Clifford R. Kreismer

Parker Publishing Company, Inc.   West Nyack, N. Y.

© 1972 by
Parker Publishing Company, Inc.
West Nyack, N. Y.

Library of Congress
Catalog Card Number: 70–172885

Printed in the United States of America
ISBN-0-13-259721-7
B&P

About the Authors:

DR. EUGENE J. BRADFORD has been teacher, high school principal, district principal, superintendent of schools, and college instructor. He has contributed many articles to professional magazines. He was awarded the "Distinguished Service Award" by the Graduate School of Education at Rutgers University; he was also the recipient of an acknowledgement award for his early work in establishing classes for neurologically impaired children in the State of New Jersey, as well as an award for his innovative activities in the creation of the New Jersey Educational Television Corporation.

Dr. Bradford created and organized the National School Boards Publications Awards, sponsored by *School Management* Magazine. He has been President of the New Jersey School Development Council, Vice President of the N. E. Region of the National School Public Relations Association, and Editorial Advisor of *Education, U. S. A.*

DR. ALBERT F. DOREMUS, a former elementary teacher, principal, and coordinator of instruction, has spent twenty years working in and writing about the elementary school field. As early as 1957, he achieved national attention for his contributions to the field of international comparison of pupil achievement. An authority on the standardized testing programs employed by the schools of the United Kingdom, Dr. Doremus established a basis for comparison between the American school product and his British counterpart.

Most recently, Dr. Doremus headed a team which revised the various elementary masters degree programs at Paterson State College, making them more functional and relative to present-day training needs. He was also a recipient of the "Founders Day Award" from New York University for high scholastic achievement.

DR. CLIFFORD R. KREISMER was the first to direct a district-wide school evaluation in New Jersey. He has also served on teams selected to assess schools following their self-evaluations. His background includes extensive elementary and secondary school teaching, a directorship of multi-media instruction, elementary principal, and administrative assistant to the superintendent. He has coordinated curriculum studies, initiated enrichment projects, and directed summer schools, adult education and international student exchange programs.

For more than a decade, Dr. Kreismer has conducted courses and seminars at colleges and universities in the areas of curriculum, child development and instructional media. He is frequently a speaker at educational conferences and a contributor of articles for professional journals. His additional writings include in-service teacher training booklets and teacher recruitment literature. Listed in *Who's Who in the East,* Dr. Kreismer is widely known as a resource person in the area of elementary school evaluation.

Foreword

When Socrates was requested to drink the fatal hemlock because of his insistence that the "life which is unexamined is not worth living," he made vivid a truth that is as pertinent to educational institutions, regardless of their level, as it is to individuals.

It is traditional in the United States for high schools, both public and private, to undergo an evaluation process, usually at ten-year intervals, in which their own related personnel and a visiting team from an accrediting organization attempt to assess the degree of effectiveness with which they fulfill the objectives implicit in their own expressed philosophy.

Because high schools have found such assessments helpful in the self-improvement process, it has become fairly common for junior high schools to seek similar evaluative experiences. But for elementary schools the practice has been infrequent, even rare.

The three authors of this book have long been interested in the evaluative process as a self-improvement aid. For a period of years they worked as an extremely successful administrative team in the same New Jersey school district. During those years they examined, through self-evaluation and outside teams, all segments of the entire school system: the high school, the junior high school, and the elementary schools. This was the first time an entire school district had been evaluated in total detail in New Jersey's history—and I believe its pioneering venture has never since been duplicated.

The authors believe sincerely that elementary schools—like secondary schools—can find educational profit in assessment. They believe in self-evaluation as a most effective in-service project. They believe, too, that the total process can be designed to obtain dividends in community support, greater clarity of objectives, school-community relationships, acceptance of anticipated directions, and sympathetic understanding of problems.

Assessment practices in elementary schools are still in their embryonic stages, and hence offer rich experimental opportunities for enterprising educators. The desired harvest, slanted to meet the specific current needs of a school, can and should be custom-tailored.

With the publication of this book, the authors have made a significant contribution to educational literature. They open up, vividly and comprehensively, a set of channels through which faculty, administration, community—yes, and students—can jointly move toward the attainment of the potentialities they envision.

Thomas E. Robinson
President Emeritus
Glassboro State College
Glassboro, N. J.

The What, Who and How
of School Evaluation

This book is written for experienced educators who, knowing of the value of elementary school assessment, require only the procedural guidelines for their schools' evaluation. Accordingly, the authors have addressed themselves to the questions of what to evaluate, where to place the emphasis, who performs the evaluation tasks, and how to reap the benefits. The selection of evaluative criteria is fully discussed. Examples of existing instruments ready to be used are included.

The busy school administrator, believing strongly in self-evaluation, finds here a pattern he can follow for organizing his staff for this introspective enterprise. Responsibilities of all involved personnel are outlined and their work schedules are suggested.

Experienced elementary principals may wish to lead the way by conducting a self-evaluative process in their own schools. For these enterprising educators, this alternative to a multi-building evaluation is explored step-by-step.

The authors, drawing upon their own experiences, have included ample "how to" material for the selection of an outside evaluation team. Answers are suggested as to the composition of the group, their care and feeding, and how they can best meet with the staff and community. Again, a sample timetable is available to aid the evaluators in their work. Ideas are offered for effective distribution of findings to the important groups within the district. Other positive public relations steps that can be taken are given in detail. Specific benefits of the entire procedure are given for the superintendent and principal. Also included are procedures to translate reports into practical application for teachers, board of education and community.

With the tasks before them larger than ever, America's elementary schools need to have the support of their communities as they rise to meet the challenge. The evaluation processes, as detailed in this book, focus just this kind of essential attention on the elementary schools. They need not remain aside as the secondary schools routinely bathe in the evaluation spotlight. The status of elementary education in a school or school district can be raised significantly in the eyes of the members of the school board, parents, and community as a result of the appraisal experience. Teachers also will undergo the most complete in-service training possible as they identify their strengths and weaknesses and make recommendations for improving instruction. The book forces, with new clarity, an examination of the aims and objectives of the curriculum.

The authors sincerely hope that principals, superintendents and other administrators will find this reference volume to be of major assistance in improving elementary schools and in gaining solid community support.

Eugene J. Bradford
Albert F. Doremus
Clifford R. Kreismer

Table of Contents

2   Selecting the Evaluative Instrument 33

Divided into the following five categories, this chapter includes
examples of different kinds of criteria illustrating various aspects
of the evaluation criteria instrument.

            Approaching the Administration — 132
            Facing the Faculty — 132
            Organizing for Self-Evaluation — 133
            Seeking Criteria — 133
            Establishing a Timetable — 133
            Teacher Participation — 134
            Self-Study Activities — 135
            Additional Self-Study Methods — 138
            The Principal's Role — 138
            Sharing Ideas — 139
            Informing the Board — 139
            Preparing the Final Report — 140
            Summer Planning — 140
            Final Report Format — 141
            The Faculty Reviews Their Work — 141
            Acting Upon Recommendations — 142
            Board of Education Involvement — 142
            Reaction to Self-Inquiry — 143

5   The Visiting Team: Its Composition and Organization 145

            Self-Generated Programs — 145
            Composition of the Visiting Team — 146
            Identification and Selection of Team Members — 147
            Likely Sources of Chairmen and Team Members — 148
            Orientation of the Team — 148
            Team Organization — 149
            The Visiting Team's Relationship to
                    the Number and Size of Schools — 150
            Background Materials Vital to the Team's Function — 150
            Timing the Distribution to Team Members — 150
            The Standard Background Materials Packet — 151
            Summary — 152

6   The Visiting Team at Work 153

            Preparatory Activities — 154
            Meeting Areas — 154
            Principal's Availability — 154
            Accommodations for the Evaluators — 155
            Visitors' Arrival — 155
            "Kick-Off" Dinner — 155
            Guidelines for the Observers — 156

Elementary School Evaluation:
Administrator's Guide to Accountability

1

What to Evaluate

The question of "what to look for in evaluation" is a critical one for the school district to answer. The answer, and the organization of the answer, to this question sets the tone and scope of the evaluation. One very common method is that used by the Association for the Evaluation of the Elementary School in their guide for Self-Appraisal and Improvement of Elementary Schools.[1] This guide is divided into five parts: Administration and Organization, Instructional Program and Materials, School Staff, School Plant, and School-Community Relations.

GUIDE OF THE ASSOCIATION FOR EVALUATION OF THE ELEMENTARY SCHOOL

The Administration and Organization section of this guide covers such areas as: the organization of the school; staff employment; in-service education; evaluation of teachers. The Instructional Program and Materials section includes such features as: development of objectives; curriculum development; subject field studies; school library; evaluation of pupil achievement and providing for individual differences. The School Staff part of the guide contains such items as: quantity and quality of the teaching staff; special teachers and consultants; qualifications and functions of the principal; supervisory practices. The School Plant section has such areas as school site; maintenance; safety and sanitation features; custodial and operational services; and the communication system. The last section deals with: policies and responsibilities for school-community relations; collecting information; involvement of laymen; using community resources; staff participation; and informing people of the community about school programs.

THREE CLASSIFICATIONS OF THE EVALUATION GUIDE

This type of guide mixes quantity and quality items together. It combines the inventory, the factual data material of the school with the evaluation of the program

---

[1]Guide for Self-Appraisal and Improvement of Elementary Schools, 1967, The Upper Midwest Regional Educational Laboratories, Inc., St. Paul, Minnesota.

and the learning process. Included is some goal and objective achievement detail. It is possible and it may be more beneficial to organize the guide into functional areas. If all the above material were to be placed on the blackboard and then classified by function, three general groupings would probably emerge. One would be that of physical standards, quantitative items; the second grouping would include the pupil learning process, the "how" of the school process; the third classification would be "how well" do we do things, the qualitative look.

QUANTITATIVE DATA—PHYSICAL PLANT—EDUCATIONAL MATERIAL

The collection of data of a quantitative nature is a very common feature of evaluation. This data may be compulsory to collect in order to meet the standards of the county or state certification or accreditation. The physical plant is usually examined as to the size of the school grounds, the square footage of the classrooms, the number and size of classrooms and special purpose areas, kind and type of seating, sanitary facilities and other details of the building. Very often the material collected will include the number and publication dates of books in the library and the classrooms, the kind and nature of the professional and resource books and whether single or multiple texts are used. The data inventory may also include the characteristics of the school staff, the administration as to number, sex, experience, and training. The nature of the community is almost always included in the data collection. Typical items would include: the age, education and ethnic nature of the population, an enrollment and growth projection. Special material that would influence the nature or size of the schools would also be included.

INSTRUCTIONAL EQUIPMENT

Instructional equipment is quite easily inventoried and is often quite important to the evaluation process. The scope and variety of instructional aids and equipment can be of great significance. Audio-visual equipment is one of the obvious areas to inventory. Not only are the number, age, and variety of the equipment important but also utilization of the instruments. The number of teachers using the equipment, the extent of each teacher's use and the purpose of the use are of major importance in the collection of data. It is obvious that equipment not in use or in use by only a few of the faculty must be noted. Special equipment such as reading pacers, timers, audiometers, should not be overlooked. The various special departments such as music, physical education and art will usually have equipment that must be included in the inventory.

"PROCESS" EVALUATION GUIDE

Many administrators and teachers will say that the "nuts and bolts," the physical inventory type of information, is really not that important. They would state that there is great agreement on the goals and objectives of the school and on the program of studies. The above individuals also would say that the philosophy of education has been understood by the faculty and community. They wish to place the emphasis of the evaluation on the "process," the "how," of what goes on in the school. They would emphasize the implementation of the program of studies, the "way" the teachers instruct the pupils, the interaction of the pupils and teachers. Great stress would be placed on the way the various pieces of instructional equipment are used, the variety and creativeness of utilization of instructional aids, the inventiveness of pupil-made and teacher-made devices. Particular attention would be given to the extent and scope of pupil-teacher, pupil-pupil, teacher-principal, and faculty-principal planning. Attention would be placed on the type of teacher instructional activity, the extent and percentage of the teacher "talk" versus the pupil "talk." Notice would be given to the variety and inventiveness of techniques that the teacher employs to individualize the instructional program. Of concern to the staff would be the scope of the individualization, whether or not all the program areas were covered or only the academic areas.

Another school of thought is that neither the "inventory" nor the "process" point of emphasis is really important. The thrust and impact of the evaluation in that instance would be on the objectives to be reached. Equal stress would be placed on the achievement of the stated goals. Planning, both long and short range, would be examined. The differentiation between the objectives and the goals of the school would need to be clearly specified. The basic question of what kind of goals would need to be exactly stated in the evaluation material. If achievement goals are to be used, the following questions will arise: Will these goals be stated in the form of age and grade standards? Will norms that have been locally developed be used? If so, what was the norming procedure, what was the norming population? In other words, was the local norm statistically and accurately developed? Will national, regional, or state norms be used? Will individualized goals for achievement be used making allowance for basic intelligence? A fundamental problem in the use of objective achievement standards is that the standard often does not measure goals that the staff deem vital.

The behavioral goals for each subject and the pupils in general are viewed by many teachers and principals as the truly important aspect of the school's hopes and desires.

The evaluation of the school should look for specific outcomes of the elementary program in terms of performance of behavioral competence and not only in terms of specific, factual knowledge. This is not to say that concrete information is not essential to the learning process but that the eventual use of that detail, the outcome of the process is where the real emphasis of evaluation should be placed.

BEHAVIORAL GOALS

The Russell Sage Foundation published the "Elementary School Objectives: A Report Prepared for the Mid-Century Committee on Outcomes in Elementary Education."

A review of some of the detailed objectives will indicate that some are very specific, while others are broad, abstract, sometimes very vague. These terms are sometimes expressive of a value, sometimes of growth and development and sometimes of difficulty. They are the outcomes that contain expressions such as "improves," "grows," "begins," or makes progress in.[2]

The report contains specific goals that are used for illustrative purposes. Some of these represent a cluster of items, while others are used to point out goals that are broadly inclusive in nature or suggestive of unnamed items. The former can be seen in, "The pupil should be able to answer such questions as: What happens to water vapor when it becomes hail? What makes the hail fall? Why do we have dew in the morning?" The latter can be seen in the response to, "He should use simple tools correctly, for their intended purposes."

The "essentials," the "fundamentals," the "subject matter content" are contained in many of the goal statements. Other goals refer to broad generalizations, understandings, habits of work, social attitudes, and others of a like kind.

The goal statements that are illustrated in the previous and following paragraphs contain the essence of where the emphasis of the evaluation must be placed, for each outcome—broad, specific, general, itemized, or however stated—must be planned for in the development of the criteria. It will be difficult in some instances to prove, to find out, if the aims have been achieved. However, it just will not suffice for the school to say that these behavioral outcomes are not measurable, cannot be determined, do not lend themselves to determinable results. If the school that is geared to this philosophy does not develop its own evaluation procedure, then it will be left up to the visiting committee to devise a schemata of its own. The visiting committee may not agree with the criteria, may think they are not applicable, not pertinent, but that is quite a different matter than not having a plan for the evaluation of the program.

Some of the itemized goals refer to memorized responses while others refer to insights and understandings not emphasizing the remembered facts. The difference can be seen in such an item as, "He can recite the alphabet from 'A to Z'," contrasted with, "He knows four different ways to classify data." There are also items that demand the ability to use knowledge in a constructive manner when meeting new situations and problems. The latter may be seen on the primary level in, "He employs experimental procedures in solving real life problems around him dealing with the care of animal pets, of making a snare for small animals, of finding out what liquids mix together, or what is the temperature at which water expands."

Some of the items in the goal statements emphasize social or group skills, while others differentiate between the capacities and potentialities of the child as an individual. Some of the outcomes are readily identifiable in terms of the conventional subjects taught in the elementary school while others are not easy to identify with any single or specific subject area.[3]

---

[2] Kearny, Nolan C., Elementary School Objectives. Russell Sage Foundation, New York 1953.

[3] Op. Cit., Pg. 46, 47.

GUIDES FOR SPECIAL TYPES OF SCHOOLS

In deciding what to look for in evaluation, schools that are organized in non-traditional ways must be given special attention. The non-graded school, the multi-age school, the combination school, the Montessori school are examples of types of schools that need careful examination in order for the unique character of the school to be noted and considered. The very special hopes, the very specialized purposes, and the very carefully unstructured and structured programs must be reflected in the evaluation criteria and procedure.

MULTI-AGE SCHOOL

The multi-age school is so organized that at least two and usually three different age groups of pupils are in the same classroom together. A typical class would have six, seven and eight year old children with the same classroom teacher. Normally these same children would be in a "first," "second," or "third" grade classroom rather than together all day. The evaluation criteria should indicate the special benefits that are supposed to accrue to the pupils in this atypical classroom grouping.

The proponents of the multi-age classroom state that this organization should enhance the opportunities for learning through social interaction. They also claim that it would also provide a richer and more varied social environment for learning. The naturally varied and the chronologically varied personalities in the classroom would, they say, stimulate and challenge the individual student's thinking. It would allow him to seek security and common interests in keeping with his own stage of development. His friends and working companions will be comprised of a variety of maturity levels dependent upon the particular activity in progress.

The multi-age environment naturally provides more opportunities for some desired kinds of social behavior to occur. The pupils have a chance to observe, be a part of, talk about, analyze, and discuss the normal problems of personality development.

Younger children in the multi-age class pass through the less mature stages to the more sophisticated. The pupils frequently gain satisfaction from the knowledge of their own positive development and are therefore more understanding of the continuousness of growth.

The National Education Association booklet entitled "Multi-Age Grouping,"[4] contains a most concise statement of the objectives, advantages, and procedures for this type of classroom organization.

> In multi-age groups each youngster can achieve his developmental tasks in a world of varied task attainment. He can see himself moving from a less mature pattern of behavior.
>
> In multi-age classrooms, day by day, each year, individuals work at their own pace on

---

[4]Multi-Age Grouping–National Education Association 1968. Washington, D. C. 20036.

their own interests and no one has to wait a year to learn what he is anxious to know now. Soon the young ones are exploring with older children and the older ones are identifying more complex problems for their independent pursuit.

Values of the multi-age approach show up in almost each event of the day in every learning situation. These values inhere in the child's development and provide an atmosphere of such positive growth that self-concepts for each child cannot help but be good.

And what of the skills! It is amazing how much children can learn from other children when there is freedom to learn. Our observations and experience with multi-age grouping have made this very clear.

Certainly there is enough evidence to affirm the value of multi-age grouping for instructional purposes until we can venture into even newer ways of organizing our schools.

Observational techniques to determine whether or not these aims are being achieved are at best incomplete. However, it is necessary that some procedure be present in the evaluation process to investigate these claims. In the next chapter more detailed instructions will be given as to the preparation of criteria that will reflect various points of emphasis that the school deems important.

UNGRADED SCHOOL

A second widely employed organization plan is that of the ungraded school. It has as its most important feature the freedom of the individual child to progress at his own rate. The pupil is not bound by the usual rigid class organization and can freely move with, ahead of, or behind the rest of the class in each subject area. It is thus possible for a student to be in one class group in reading, in another in arithmetic, and in a third and still different group in science. With the child setting the pace for progress and movement, the usual time period for advancement from grade to grade is eliminated, since there are no grades. There are only groupings of pupils that are non-permanent, always changing.

Many schools achieve partial nongradedness by grouping pupils according to progress only in one or two subject areas such as reading and arithmetic. The rest of the day the pupils are in their own conventional class group. Progress is also measured by the year, and first grade, second grade exist as firm classifications.

PUPIL-TEACHER PLANNING

The ungraded and the multi-age school share one very important feature that the evaluation criteria must reflect. This is the amount and quality of teacher-pupil planning. For these programs to be successful, this planning must be highly individualized for each child. It should reflect the child's very personal interests, his unique capacities, his individual learning style. The difficulty of formulating criteria for the multi-age and non-graded school may be very quickly apparent to the faculty and administration. This very real problem should not lead to the overlooking or elimination of the vital distinctions of these schools. In the preparation of the criteria for these special features of the different schools the faculty and administration will truly gain in deep understanding of their uniqueness.

MONTESSORI AND WALDORF SCHOOLS

Specialized schools such as the Montessori and the Waldorf pose unique problems in the development of the evaluation instrument. The central purpose, the educational philosophy, the process implementation, the true "heart and soul" of the individual school must be reflected in criteria of the self-evaluation document. While this may sound to be true of any and all schools, and this is correct, it has impressive significance in the case of the specialty schools named above.

The Montessori schools follow the methods, practices, and philosophy of Dr. Maria Montessori, the noted Italian educator. To attempt to use the typical public school and its standards of procedure and practices as a model of evaluation for this highly different school would be a tragic mistake. It would also defeat the purpose of evaluation which is to use the philosophy of the school to be evaluated as the key to the evaluation, not the experience or the viewpoint of the evaluator. Indeed, it is one of the functions of the chairman of the evaluation team to warn his committee members about this peril to a truly fair and objective evaluation.

OBSERVING THE CHILD

Dr. Montessori stressed that she developed her methods of instruction by observing the children at work and play. She then formulated her theories from this observational data bank. She did not first elaborate a theory of instruction and build a set of practices on that theory. This matter of observing the child very closely is one of the key features of the Montessori school. However, to this feature of close observation is added that of allowing the child to proceed naturally with the task at hand. The direction, scope, and duration of the work is left to the individual pupil to determine. Teacher assistance is freely given when requested but is not forcibly imposed on the person. The teacher may suggest tasks that are increasingly difficult. However, the individual child is the one who determines whether or not the task is germane and manageable.

DISCIPLINE

The matter of discipline is another distinctive difference about the Montessori school. The bedrock of the school's philosophy on this matter is that there shall be no unnecessary compulsion used to get the pupil to do anything and that there be continuous recognition of the second part of the definition of discipline—the capacity for self-control. Self-control and compulsion are opposites that do not fit together in the matter of development of Montessori school disciplinary practices.

EVALUATOR MUST UNDERSTAND PHILOSOPHY OF SCHOOL

The evaluator must look for examples of the way this philosophy is carried out and exemplified. The liberty of action given in these schools is not a reflection of total, unrestrained freedom. It insists that the rights of all other pupils be recognized and not interfered with. It further believes that this is the ideal way to train for true democracy. The school does not sanction license but does give the pupil a chance to work out the limits of his own action. Since this is a most unusual and different phase of the school operation, it must be specially provided for in the self-evaluation activity. There are many other distinctions about the Montessori schools that have not been mentioned, but these will of course be noted in the material given to the visiting committee.

THE WALDORF SCHOOL—ANOTHER EXAMPLE

The Waldorf school is another example of a school that has a quite definite philosophy of education that is exemplified in the operation of the school. Much of what the philosophy states is not new or particularly original in itself. It is the totality, the pulling together of many elements of education in a new way that makes for a different school. The new combination, the new mix of points of emphasis, is what makes each school, and the Waldorf school in particular, unique. Waldorf stresses some of the same practices of the Montessori schools, namely, self-discipline, concern for the other student, and responsibility for one's own intellectual development.

WALDORF EDUCATIONAL PHILOSOPHY

For example, reading does not precede but follows the practice of writing. First comes the action, then the recognition. Through speech, then through writing, language is created. Through hearing and through reading it is perceived. In life generally, and in Waldorf education, creation comes first and then the beholding, the onlooking, the appreciation. This school endeavors to reach these goals and others by quite different methods and processes. The very difficult task for the evaluation committee is the job of assessing the outcome of the school in terms of its own declared objectives, particularly when the aims are not those of the usual public or private school. The self-evaluation must reflect and pay especial attention to the uniqueness of the school in its deliberations. It should give many examples to establish the outcomes, to prove that its philosophy is being carried out by the school. The visiting committee will need all the help that can be provided to continually keep in mind and focus the unique features of the school as it does its review of the school.[5]

---

[5]Gardner, John F., The Experience of Knowledge. The Myrin Institute, Inc., 521 Park Avenue, New York, 10021.

The private country day school is another example of a special school that needs particular attention when the self-evaluation material is constructed. Many of these schools make claims about their uniqueness in their parent prospectus booklets. These statements range from highly individualized instruction, attention to each student's needs, personalized instruction, with each statement emphasizing the same thing—the individual student is all-important, and instruction is adapted to the particular student. They also usually state that the school will prepare the student for college, enable him to learn the methods and techniques of studying and a great many other beneficial procedures. The evaluation criteria should reflect and prove the claims, aims, and goals that the individual school states, whether in the printed material for prospective pupils and parents or in the official material prepared for the evaluation committee.

SCHOOLS FOR THE HANDICAPPED

In addition to these schools with their particular philosophy of education, there are other schools that have special pupils, unique pupils, as their element of difference from the typical school. These are the schools for pupils who are physically or mentally handicapped, or are emotionally disturbed. The special problem of each group of pupils and the creativeness of the educational process in reaching each child to enable him to overcome his difficulty must be a part of the self-evaluation.

In schools for the physically handicapped, the physical aspects of the school will be of great importance. The self-evaluation must be extensive and complete on the ramps, handholds, railings, adaptive furniture, special lighting, and other features that are specially provided for the students. Equal attention must be given to the safety precautions and procedures that the school provides. Fire doors, emergency provisions, exit safe-guards and the like should be carefully noted. Where the handicap is specific, such as deafness or blindness, the self-evaluation must be equally specific in its description of the adaptations the school makes for these handicaps. A practical matter often overlooked is the process of getting the student to school. This can be particularly difficult for some forms of physical handicap, such as cerebral palsy. The details of how this is accomplished should be part of every self-evaluation.

SCHOOLS FOR THE EMOTIONALLY DISTURBED STUDENT

The emotionally disturbed student is another example of the special pupil that must have particularly planned school facilities. All entrances and exits should have simple, uncomplicated, ready-to-operate hardware. The furniture should be mar-proof and sturdy. Provisions for large-activity classwork must also be provided. This type of need-provision for the student is easy to ascertain by the visiting committee and should not create any difficulty in creating the self-evaluation instrument.

The emotionally disturbed student does not always need any physically different classroom or school. The climate and the general aura of the school is the most important aspect for the student. The use of such words as "climate" and "aura" when they are a critical part of the school create difficult problems in the development of the evaluation instrument. How does one "prove" or "account for" or "show evidence of" such intangibles? One way would be to focus on the process. However, this will be more explicitly developed in the next chapter.

In the schools for the handicapped, a most critical point for the evaluation group to consider is the ability of the staff to make the pupil feel that he is worthy of being alive, that he is an important member of the total child group, that his rights and needs are as important as those of "normal" children. This area of ego nourishment, of positive self-concept development, should be present in abundance in these schools. In fact, it can be said that the schools will not be successful unless the staff views this psychological re-enforcement and build-up as fundamental and critical, in addition to the physiological needs of the students.

INDIVIDUALIZATION OF INSTRUCTION

Since most of these children are in very small classes, the individualization of instruction should be readily apparent to the evaluator. This aspect of the learning process must be carefully examined since it is one of the principal reasons for legally restricted small-class size. The needs of the pupils are so highly different from one another that individually planned work should be the hallmark of the daily routine. This is to be distinguished from the class activity that is planned to make the pupils feel a sense of togetherness and mutual respect. The inventiveness of the teachers in reaching each child and processing the learning material should also be reflected in the evaluation criteria.

In these schools for special children, the amount and quality of the parent communication process must also be a feature of the criteria. Most parents of handicapped children are understandably anxious and apprehensive about their children. The school should have highly developed parent-information, and indeed, parent-discussion programs. These programs will assist the parents to begin to ease their tensions so they can then more easily help their children to cope with the handicap.

IMPORTANCE OF PHILOSOPHY OF EDUCATION

In the preceding material of this chapter, attention has been placed on the distinguishing features of various types of school organization and pupil populations. The answer to the question, "What should one look for in evaluation?" is contained in the very stated uniqueness of the school. This is usually contained in the school's philosophy statement which is critical and essential as a part of the evaluation material that is furnished to the evaluation group. This credo of the school should be clear and unequivocal in its broad goals and in the statement of realizable objectives. A common mistake of the faculty and administration is to view this philosophy statement as not really important. They sometimes act as though this part of the evaluation need only be given perfunctory attention. On the contrary, this is the "rock" on which the whole school functions; this is the unifying force for teachers and administrators. This is what gives a sense of direction to the school. It provides the "heading" for the voyage of the pupils through the school. It is through these "eyes" that the evaluators view the school. This is the common point of reference for the evaluation process.

It has been repeatedly stated that the fundamental starting point of all evaluation is the philosophy of the individual school that is being evaluated. This statement of purpose and direction is the standard to which all the evaluation material is referred. This direction of the school is to be developed first by the school and used as the reference point for the self-study by the faculty. All questions arising about the process, procedure or operation of the evaluation should be constantly measured against the philosophy of the school.

PURPOSE OF PHILOSOPHY

Another vexing problem for the faculty to overcome is the purpose of the evaluation. Such questions continually arise as to what the evaluation is to point out, what is the point of emphasis of the self-study, why list all the inventory-type material, why show process if goals are to be stressed, why do any list making when all we are really interested in is success in achieving our stated objectives, why not do only the material that the state department asks for and nothing more, why not do just the necessary work and nothing more. Questions such as these are endless and are typically raised by all faculties in their preliminary discussions about the entire self-evaluation procedure. Essentially, this is a problem of distinguishing between ends and means, between purpose and result. If the questions are put into this simple light it may assist the group in answering this dilemma. The group can state for example: "We are primarily interested in getting past the State Department of Education review and receiving our official approval. We do not want to do anything more." If the self-evaluation criteria do not contain any material on process or behavioral goals, then these items will not be included in the evaluation review. The question of whether the school should do more than the minimum is another entirely different matter.

IMPORTANCE OF SCHOOL'S PHILOSOPHY TO ACHIEVE RESULTS

Another school may decide that it wishes to examine in great depth the success it has in meeting goals that have already been stated and accepted by the faculty and community. This school would have quite different criteria than the first school cited. The emphasis in this school would be on the successful achievement of objectives. The product, the result, judged by the standard of the school's own philosophy, should dominate the self-evaluation procedure. The evaluative criteria should abound in items that measure. This measurement may be either subjective or objective but it will attempt to state output of the school in terms of the stated philosophy. The criteria may contain such items as: test results; local, regional, or state norms; percentile rankings of the class or individual student result in certain examinations; behavioral goal attainment in specific subject areas; attitudinal changes. There will be small emphasis on such material as lists of equipment, inventories, size of rooms, acreage of grounds.

A faculty may decide to work from the premise that these are the things that they think are important, that they wish to examine, that they want to review in depth. From these items will naturally develop the purpose of the evaluation. In other words, the group started from the item analysis to purpose, from the particular to the general. Other schools may reverse the process and begin with the general purpose statement and then proceed to the items that will fulfill that purpose.

WHO SETS THE STANDARDS?

The question of who makes what decisions is usually decided locally. In many communities the central decision of having the elementary schools evaluated is made by the central office or by the board of education. The impetus for the study may have come from the board of education because it had a certification or accreditation mandate to fulfill. In some states, the elementary schools must be regularly evaluated at stated intervals. In these cases the standards for the evaluation and the evaluation criteria are also set forth in detail. The next chapter will illustrate examples of the forms and the criteria that are used in some states. Many of the state evaluation procedures and criteria that have been examined show a naturally heavy emphasis on the mandated items of state control. Material such as the size of the classrooms, the acreage of the school site, safety features of fire exits, fire extinguishers, certification of teachers employed, number of staff members, are usually stressed. In addition to these types of items the evaluation contains many items that tend to show that certain processes are being carried out, i.e., developing and maintaining optimum physical health and fitness, using related art experiences to define and understand one's self. The question of how well or how extensively these process items are being carried out is rarely indicated in the criteria.

Occasionally the impetus for the evaluation is made at the local school, or individual school level. This usually results from the principal's desire to improve his school and using the evaluation process as the vehicle to accomplish that purpose. One school in a multiple-school district may at times be selected to be a pilot school in a study of elementary school evaluation.

PRESSURE FOR EVALUATION

At times, pressure may be the reason for the evaluation to take place. The pressure may be of many forms and for a variety of reasons. The local parent-teacher association may want the schools examined because they feel they are not educating their children well, or because the schools are on double sessions and they want a new school. The teacher association may want the evaluation to support a contention that some aspect of the system is not performing well, or that the total system is not functioning as it should. Individual groups such as the elementary principals may also have similar aims and request an evaluation to support their claims. When pressure of whatever form is the compelling reason for the evaluation, the principal emphasis of the criteria will be the objectives of the pressure group.

SUMMARY

A decision to evaluate the schools may be the result of many influences all wishing to use the evaluation for the same purpose or for different purposes. For example, the board of education, superintendent, citizens' groups, teachers, may all wish to have the evaluation to sincerely point out areas of needed improvement in the school programs. There may not be any preconceived idea that there is necessarily any weakness at all, just a true desire to periodically assess the progress of the schools. Opposed to this idealistic viewpoint is the reverse situation, that of each group having its own independent idea of why to evaluate the schools. The board of education may wish to prove the need for additional schools, the central office the need for more specialists, the teachers to prove that the class size and teacher load is too heavy for good instruction, and the citizens' group that the community needs are not being met. The ideal solution to diverse reasons for the evaluation is to bring together representatives of all the groups and to cooperatively work out the details of the criteria so that each need is thoroughly assessed by the evaluative criteria. If any group feels that its wants are not sufficiently covered in the evaluation, it will create a damaging blow to the ready acceptance of the results of the evaluation besides making a vital part of the community either hostile or indifferent to the very process of the evaluation. To be truly successful, each group must feel that its particular needs and aims are being met.

In some instances, the evaluation is initiated by the central office when a new superintendent takes charge. The purposes in these instances are usually to provide a base for future comparisons, to furnish an assessment of the present condition of the school achievement. Short and long range programs of improvement can then be better formulated for the system. If the program is undertaken with an honest attempt to perceive the present condition of the schools and not to denigrate a predecessor superintendent or board of education, then acceptance of the evaluation is usually assured. The faculty and administration must be fully apprised of this vital professional purpose in order for them to cooperate completely in the evaluation. What is being emphasized in these statements is the necessity for complete honesty, true professionalism on the part of the designers of the evaluation criteria, which must always reflect the diversity of the various interest groups.

2

Selecting the
Evaluative Instrument

If you don't ask the right questions, you won't get the correct answers. This truism is especially pertinent to the selection and development of the evaluation instrument. It is through the evaluation instrument, the details sought, the questions asked, the information requested, the data compiled, that the true being, the real essence of the school will be revealed. In this chapter there will be given many examples of the different kinds of criteria, for many different purposes, from different sources. This will enable the administrator or teacher group seeking to undertake an elementary school evaluation to select from a variety of examples upon which to build the local school criteria.

Examples will be given from professional administrator groups such as: The Minnesota Elementary Principals Association, university-connected sources as represented by the New Jersey School Development Council, various state departments of education in different areas of the country, national accrediting associations including the Middle States Association of Colleges and Secondary Schools of the National Study of Secondary School Evaluation, individual school systems, and national groups such as the Association for the Evaluation of the Elementary Schools.

Material has been selected from these sources to *illustrate* various aspects of the evaluation criteria instrument. *It is not intended to be a complete list of items that would be included in an evaluation criteria booklet.* In some cases, only highlights of some of the criteria are illustrated. Several examples of the same part of the instrument will be given to show the variety of ways to answer the same problem.

Although there are many ways to organize the complete evaluation instrument, this chapter will follow the guide for "Self-Appraisal and Improvement of Elementary Schools" of the Association for the Evaluation of the Elementary School, because it is complete, all inclusive, and it is produced by a professional group specifically concerned with the elementary school evaluation. This guide has five sections: Administration and Organization of the School; Instructional Program and Materials; School Staff; School Plant; School-Community Relations. Within these divisions it will be possible to give many examples of the variety of procedures followed by different groups to evaluate the various aspects of the elementary school. There will be brief explanations of the criteria examples illustrated, either on the same page or on the facing page. In addition the source of the illustration is credited so that inquiry can be made for additional information, if so desired. A section on Organizing the Guide precedes the sections listed above in order to assist administrators.

Organizing the Guide

---

*The Tables of Contents illustrated will enable the administrator or teacher group to note quickly the scope and nature of the material existing in evaluation guides. It will be noted that the guides are of diverse lengths and complexity; however, some consistency is apparent in the material of the guides. There is also great flexibility of content to meet the various purposes of the states and organizations.

Guide for Self-Appraisal and Improvement
of Elementary Schools

Evaluative Criteria

CONTENTS

Prepared by The Association for Evaluation of The Elementary
School and Disseminated by The Upper Midwest Regional
Educational Laboratory, Inc., 2698 University Avenue,
St. Paul, Minnesota 55114.

This publication was prepared persuant to a Contract with the
United States Department of Health, Education and Welfare,
Office of Education.

Authors' Note: This is the format of the Association for the Evaluation of the Elementary
School, which is perhaps the only extant organization specifically organized to evaluate the elementary schools. The format is typical, contains the usual chapter or section headings, and gives a good
coverage of the standard items in elementary evaluative criteria.

Manual for Evaluative Criteria

Contents of Evaluative Criteria

Foreword

Contents of Manual

EVALUATIVE CRITERIA
Fourth Edition

by National Study of Secondary School Evaluation, *1785 Massachusetts Avenue, N.W., Washington, D.C. 20036. All rights reserved. No part of this material may be reproduced in any form without prior written permission of the publisher.*

Authors' Note: This is from the "fountainhead," the national standard used in the accreditation of the secondary schools of the country. Even though it refers to the high school, it is a splendid example of the complete evaluation process. It could serve as a sample, with minor adaption, for the large city elementary systems or as a model from which less complete guides could be developed.

SELF–STUDY FOR ELEMENTARY SCHOOLS

TABLE OF CONTENTS

The Gloucester County Elementary School Principals'
and Supervisors' Professional Improvement Project

Published by the Office of the Gloucester County Superintendent
of Schools, County Office of Education, Clayton, New Jersey

Authors' Note: This guide is specifically for the self-study of the school by a faculty. It does not pretend to be for a visiting committee. The areas covered are not too different from the other evaluation guides.

Standards
for
Accrediting
Elementary
Schools
in Virginia

TABLE OF CONTENTS

ELEMENTARY EDUCATION SERVICE
STATE DEPARTMENT OF EDUCATION
RICHMOND, VIRGINIA 23216

Authors' Note: This guide is a typical state department of education publication dealing with evaluation. It is more nearly concerned with the accreditation of the elementary school than with the self-evaluation or critical evaluation of the process or achievements of the school.

Evaluation Manual

For the Improvement of

Elementary Schools

SECTION A.   NATURE AND PURPOSE OF THE MANUAL

According to Shane and McSwain[1], evaluation is "a process of inquiry based upon criteria cooperatively prepared and concerned with the study, interpretation, and guidance of socially desirable changes in the developmental behavior of children. Phrased in another way, evaluation is a scientific method used in determining what elementary schools can do effectively to provide a curriculum of meaningful living and learning which insures for each child maximum development through daily experiencing and also adequate preparation through his present living for the duties ultimately inherent in adult citizenship."

There are many methods of evaluating a school program. One simple and expeditious method is to call in experts from the outside to measure the effectiveness of the school in terms of arbitrary standards. Although this method is perhaps beneficial in extreme cases where local leadership has abdicated its responsibility, it fails to achieve the professional growth on the part of the local staff which comes from participation in an evaluation program.

I.   A Cooperative Approach to Evaluation

This manual has been predicated upon the belief that evaluation of any school program is basically the responsibility of the local school system. It is also based upon the belief that the extent to which evaluation actually results in improving the teaching-learning situation depends upon the extent to which the local school staff participates in the evaluation program. The manual also recognizes that, when evaluation is carried on in the light of democratic values, every one concerned with the school program—supervisors, principals, teachers, pupils, and parents—takes a part in the evaluation of the teaching-learning situation.

The persons charged with the responsibility of preparing and revising the manual recognize the contributions which can be made by experts. They believe, however, that such experts from outside the school system should be used primarily as consultants and advisors to help the local staff identify objectives, formulate programs for the achievement of those objectives, and develop procedures for evaluating objectives. Such experts should not be evaluators of the current programs.

II.   An Experimental Approach to Evaluation

According to Saylor and Alexander[2], "to evaluate is to determine the value of. The evaluation of curriculum planning is the determination of the value of that planning. Thus evaluation is one phase of the total process of curriculum planning . . . We plan the curriculum to achieve educational values. Our planning is based on evaluation of existing plans . . ."

Most authorities today are agreed that evaluation is necessary for growth and progress; yet, in many schools, evaluation is the weakest link in the entire program of educational planning. Too often faculties either lack knowledge and skill in evaluation, or their evaluations are desultory and subjective.

continued

Authors' Note: After the table of contents in the evaluation guides, the next most frequent material is some statement as to the purpose and the basic premises of the evaluation. The philosophy of the school district is usually part of these general goal statements.

The Oklahoma statement of the nature and purpose of the evaluation manual stresses the cooperative nature of the study and the benefits to be derived from the experimental approach to the evaluation. It also gives a brief idea of the purpose of evaluating elementary schools, in general.

This manual represents an attempt to help faculties of elementary schools develop a systematic, orderly, and comprehensive program for evaluating the teaching-learning situation in their own schools. The checklists in the following sections are believed to be consistent with the results of educational research and are based on the best judgment of leaders in elementary education throughout the state of Oklahoma. Thus, all items on the checklists are deemed desirable conditions or practices.

The Oklahoma State Department of Education

Evaluation Manual

For the Improvement of

Elementary Schools

The manual is flexible in that it is an open-ended instrument which provides opportunities for local staff members and citizens to identify strengths and weaknesses which may or may not be included in the checklists.

The manual is experimental in that all persons using the manual will be invited to make recommendations and suggestions to the Oklahoma Curriculum Improvement Commission for continued revision and improvement. The present manual is a revision of the experimental manual published in 1957. This revised edition is based upon criticisms and suggestions of persons who used the experimental form. It is expected that the manual will be revised periodically as suggestions and criticisms are received from the users.

III. Purposes of the Manual

The manual is designed to help the elementary schools of Oklahoma provide better programs for the children of Oklahoma. It is not a rating instrument. It is not a comparison instrument whereby one school will be compared with another.

The major purposes of the manual are:

1. To stimulate evaluation programs in the elementary schools of Oklahoma,

2. to provide a systematic, orderly, and comprehensive basis for a cooperative program of evaluation by teachers, administrators, parents, and children,

3. to provide a challenge for better educational thinking, and

4. to furnish "self" checklists to be used as a basis for in-service study and discussion which will be fruitful in producing improved curriculum and practices in the individual schools.

One additional purpose of the manual is to furnish the Oklahoma Curriculum Improvement Commission with information which will help the commission in its efforts to improve education in Oklahoma. All reports to the commission will be voluntary and may include both current evaluations and suggestions for improvement and revision of the manual.

continued

IV. How to Use the Manual

    1. The manual should be used for in-service study and discussion.

    2. No time limit should be set for completion of the manual. There is no reason to believe that the manual should be completed in one school year. Rather, each section should be studied and discussed carefully and completely. Plans should be made to improve the existing conditions and practices in the light of the evaluation. Such plans should be tried and re-evaluation made.

    3. Sufficient copies of the manual should be made available so the principal, each teacher, and at least 6 parents at each elementary school may have a copy of the manual.

    4. The person responsible for the in-service education program in the elementary schools of the school system should call a meeting of all elementary principals and all PTA presidents to discuss the purposes of the evaluation program and to make plans for it.

    5. Each elementary school should be organized as a committee of the whole to study each section of the manual and to arrive at a group evaluation for each of the items in the section. This should involve objective thinking based upon reference and research reading, not merely subjective opinion.

    6. A definite schedule for meetings should be established. Although it is not feasible to suggest any definite schedule for such meetings in every school which may engage in self-study and evaluation, well-organized meetings every other week will perhaps constitute a reasonable amount of in-service education of this type.

The Oklahoma State Department of Education

Guide for Self-Appraisal and Improvement
of Elementary Schools

Basic Premises Essential to the Achievement of

Quality in the Elementary School Program

In the development of a guide for appraising elementary schools certain basic assumptions must be made. The Basic Premises herewith presented underlie the criteria, principles and standards presented in this guide. It is assumed that these Basic Premises will be accepted by most of the people who have occasion to use this Guide.

1. Each child is entitled to every opportunity for the maximum development of his potential ability. This means mental and physical development, mental health, emotional maturity, social adjustment, and moral character.

2. Each child should acquire the skills and understandings needed to help him share the responsibilities of a democratic society. In the democratic society each individual has personal worth to the social group and should be a contributing member of his community.

3. Children differ in rate of development as well as in ability. The school accepts each child at his particular stage of development and fosters continued growth. Each child is stimulated to work at his individual maximum capacity level.

4. The school assumes responsibility for all activities connected with the school program and shares with laymen concern for the out-of-school environment which also educates the child.

5. Cooperative relationships are established between the school, the home and community in order to facilitate the fullest educational development of children and to coordinate the educational activities of the various agencies of the community.

continued

Authors' Note: This statement of basic premises is in reality a philosophy of education that underlies the evaluation process. It is by this standard that the evaluation study is to proceed.

6. Long-time goals for the school are developed cooperatively by the professional staff and lay citizens. These are revised from time to time as changes in society and needs of pupils warrant such changes. Objectives of the various learning experiences contribute toward the achievements of golas of education. Purposes in learning experiences are apparent to children.

   Such goals as are developed should include provision for: (1) literacy, (2) mental and physical health, (3) competence in human relations, (4) responsibilities of citizenship, (5) moral and spiritual values, (6) tools of learning, (7) understanding the environment, (8) skill in the use of scientific method, (9) skill in the use of numbers, (10) wise use of leisure time and (11) critical and constructive thinking.

Prepared by The Association for Evaluation of The Elementary School and Disseminated by The Upper Midwest Regional Educational Laboratory, Inc., 2698 University Avenue, St. Paul, Minnesota 55114.

This publication was prepared pursuant to a Contract with the United States Department of Health, Education and Welfare, Office of Education.

Administration and Organization of the School

EVALUATION GOVERNED BY PHILOSOPHY
AND OBJECTIVES OF INDIVIDUAL SCHOOL

The Study has developed a proved way of recognizing that schools which are quite different may be equally good. This type of evaluation is based on the principle that a school should be evaluated in terms of what it is striving to accomplish (its philosophy and objectives) and according to the extent to which it is meeting the needs of the students enrolled and of the community it serves. The philosophy and objectives must, of course, be acceptable to some agency (a community, an accrediting association, a state department of education, a board of trustees, a religious organization) if the evaluation based upon such philosophy and objectives is to be recognized beyond the confines of the school. It is obviously unfair to say that a school is of poor quality because it does not prepare students for further academic work when, in fact, it interprets its function as that of preparing youth to enter employment immediately upon graduation and to have a salable skill at that time. It is appropriate to criticize the soundness of such an objective; but if its graduates are good workmen, it is not appropriate to report that the school is of low quality. Similarly, a school can hardly be considered a good school if it is responsible for the education of all the youth in the community and yet offers a program in which only a highly selected part of the youth of that community can make satisfactory progress.

The evaluations resulting from the use of materials and procedures recommended by the National Study of Secondary School Evaluation may be considered as ratios of accomplishment where the quality and nature of work done in a school are related to what should be done in order to satisfy the philosophy and objectives of the school and the needs of the youth who are or should be served by the school. This does not make the evaluation of secondary schools a simple task: it does, however, establish a sound basis for such an evaluation.

> **EVALUATIVE CRITERIA**
> **Fourth Edition**

Authors' Note: The point of emphasis in this Secondary School example is that the evaluation must be governed by the philosophy of education of the school district under study. This was a strong point of emphasis in the preceding chapter and is repeated throughout the book.

SELF-STUDY FOR ELEMENTARY SCHOOLS

GUIDELINES FOR WRITING EVALUATIVE CRITERIA

SECTION I

PHILOSOPHY AND OBJECTIVES

The School's Philosophy

Your philosophy sets forth the basic beliefs you hold--beliefs that
justify the objectives you state. Philosophy also provides the reasons for
the ways you teach, your role as a teacher, and the role that the school plays
in the community, and the community in the school.

It may be helpful, although it sounds illogical, to start answering some
of the questions in Section I before you prepare a finished statement of
philosophy. Often we find out what we really mean and believe as we examine
what we are doing (or not doing). If, for example, a staff states that it
deeply believes in the democratic way of life, and that democratic procedures should characterize the whole school, but no regular assessment of
such procedures are made, the staff then should raise a question about the
depth of this belief. Are we as serious about democracy as about arithmetic? We usually assess achievement in arithmetic regularly.

To be repetitious, the philosophy should be your own philosophy. It is
to guide you, and you alone. Write it for yourself. Stress clarity over
literary elegance. Make it a kind of "This we believe...." type of statement.

The School's Objectives

It may be better to focus on a few central objectives in preparing the
report, rather than to develop an exhaustive list, especially so if it is
clear what each staff member understands the objective to mean in light of
children's behavior. For example, each school stresses citizenship. But
what does the staff agree that children should be demonstrating or doing if
they are gaining in citizenship? Unless this is clear, the objective is mean-
ingless as a staff objective. Similarly, what is meant by such broad and
common objectives as: healthful and safe living, good personal-social attitudes, good character, and artistic or esthetic development? It may be important to the school's growth through this evaluation to think more about
these broad and often vague objectives than about the basic skills of reading, writing, and quantitative thinking, for the latter have received considerable attention in most schools already.

Published by the Office of the Gloucester County Superintendent
of Schools, County Office of Education, Clayton, New Jersey

Authors' Note: This is one of the few examples of statements that distinguish between
philosophy and objectives. The definitions are clear and concise and would be of great help to a
faculty struggling with these two difficult concepts.

SELF–STUDY FOR ELEMENTARY SCHOOLS

ELEMENTARY SCHOOL EVALUATIVE CRITERIA

SECTION I

PHILOSOPHY AND OBJECTIVES

Section I should provide a clear statement of what the central objectives of the school are. Objectives tell what the school is trying to do; philosophy provides the reasons why the school holds these objectives. This statement is the most vital part of the evaluation, for all that the school does must be weighed against its broad objectives and philosophy. It is especially important, then, that the statement be the school's own statement; that the statement be absolutely clear and meaningful to the whole staff; and that constant reference be made to the statement in making judgments throughout Section III. (No model statement is suggested in the "Guidelines," but a few suggestions are offered.)

1. The philosophy of the school is:

2. The objectives of the school are:

Published By

The Office of the Gloucester County Superintendent of Schools
County Office of Education, Clayton, New Jersey

_____

Authors' Note: Of particular benefit is the section that gives guidelines for the writing of the objectives and philosophy. The advice is simple but most clear and useful.

Managing by
—and with—
Objectives

THE OBJECTIVE-CENTERED PERFORMANCE APPRAISAL AND REVIEW PROCESS
Aluminum Company of America

For the past several years the importance of establishing specific performance objectives has been emphasized as an essential part of Alcoa's performance appraisal and review process. Experience has indicated, however, that our Performance Appraisal and Review Form (SF-3239) does not give sufficient prominence either to the idea or the process of setting specific performance goals or objectives. As a result, a supplement to the present form has been developed—one that should help in the move from a stated objective through the planning and control phases to achievement.

A brief word should be said at this point in definition of the phrase "management by objectives." This is a method of management which emphasizes goals to be reached and in its full application calls for specific objectives to be established for each position. The goals or objectives identify the specific results to be achieved over a given period of time, usually a year. At the end of this period actual *results achieved* are measured against the original goals planned and the *results expected*. This process is derived from the sound notion that a manager should be measured by what he accomplishes. ("It's not what he does, but *what he gets done* that counts.") It is clear that as this concept is applied to a particular position it helps define in a very specific way *what the job is* in terms of *what should be accomplished*. Thus, "objectives" provide basic purpose and direction to activity. As someone has said, "If you know where you want to go, you increase your chances of getting there." And if you have a list of objectives defined in terms of "results to be achieved." you have a very solid notion of what an individual's job is.

In practice, a performance appraisal process that incorporates the management-by-objectives thinking becomes a very straightforward operation:

1. An individual writes down his *major* performance objectives for the coming year, and his specific plans (including target dates) for achieving these objectives.

2. He submits them to his boss for review. Out of the discussion comes an agreed-upon set of objectives.

3. On a quarterly basis he verbally reviews progress toward these objectives with his boss. Objectives and plans are revised and up-dated as needed.

4. At the end of the year, the individual prepares a brief "accomplishment report," which lists all major accomplishments, with comments on the variances between *results actually achieved* and the *results expected*.

5. This "self-appraisal" is discussed with the boss. Reasons for goals not being met are explored.

6. A new set of objectives is established for the next year.

With this objective-centered approach, the *principal emphasis* is on mutual planning and problem solving rather than on the production of an informed judgment of an individual's performance by his supervisor. The amount and direction of individual growth and job performance improvement are seen to be controlled largely by the quality of the *objectives* and *plans* originally agreed upon. For this reason, the actual "working-out" of objectives and plans is of critical importance to the success of the process.

NATIONAL INDUSTRIAL CONFERENCE BOARD, Inc.
845 Third Ave., New York, N. Y. 10022
Midwest Office – 120 Oakbrook Mall, Oak Brook, Ill. 60523

Authors' Note: Management by objectives is a method of operation that is being used by many business firms. The application of this method to education and to the evaluation process may bring clarity of purpose and design to the study. It is also most useful in the assessment of the administration methods and techniques that will be a part of the evaluation criteria.

Highlights FOR THE EXECUTIVE

THE MANAGEMENT-BY-OBJECTIVES concept has tremendous appeal for American businessmen, judging by the number of firms that have instituted programs and practices based upon this idea. The concept itself is simple: the clearer the idea one has of what one is trying to accomplish, the greater the chances of accomplishing it.

Many firms have installed management by objectives as a managerial performance-appraisal mechanism or have applied the idea for manpower planning or compensation purposes. Other firms have followed a more global course; in these companies management by objectives has become an approach to the total job of managing the firm. This report concentrates upon the experience of these latter companies.

Applying the Concept

In application, the complexity of managing with objectives becomes apparent. Managing with objectives requires unusually close and precise attention to the job of managing.

Step 1: Setting Objectives

Individual managers determine what specific results they plan to produce as a result of their efforts. They also carefully plan how these results will be produced, but the emphasis is on the result rather than on the means.

The objectives are stated as precisely as possible. For most firms, this means in quantitative terms whenever feasible. Finding the right measure to use with an objective has proved to be as hard as finding the right objective in the first place.

Companies have also discovered that they must ensure that the objectives of one manager merge, rather than conflict, with those of other managers who may share in the accomplishment of some larger business goal. Providing for this "interlock" of objectives has also proved difficult.

While individual managers initiate the process of setting objectives, the proposals they originate are reviewed by their bosses to ensure that subordinate goals are in support of the goals of higher levels in the organization and that, ultimately, the corporate objectives will be achieved.

This has meant, in most firms, that information about the view of the future from the top has had to be transmitted downward in the organization, so that individual managers have a meaningful context within which to formulate their goals. Companies have developed a variety of means for achieving this two-way flow of information and objectives.

Step 2: Working toward the Goals

Doing the work seems to have been the easiest part of the process. Some firms report pleasant surprise, however, at the genuine commitment which managers now bring to their work; achieving the objectives they have helped to develop seems really to matter to many managers.

Step 3: Reviewing Performance

Objectives not only serve to point effort in the right direction, they serve in measuring progress as well. This review of progress takes the form of normal managerial control, but with greater effectiveness because of clearer goals and more detailed advanced planning about how to achieve them.

The Benefits

Companies report that the greatest benefit of management by objectives is improved management. Planning is more precise and useful; control is tightened even though it tends to be self-control by the responsible manager rather than by his superiors. Relationships improve between superiors and subordinates and also between peers in different functions.

The Problems

Learning to manage with objectives effectively has proven to take most managers about two years of hard work. Further, some managers have tended to concentrate exclusively on achieving their stated objectives, allowing other aspects of their responsibilities to go slack. Finally, management by objectives has required major organization and administrative changes in many firms before its full benefits could be realized.

Case Studies

Reports on the management-by-objectives programs, and their place in the management of five companies, are included in the report. The firms are: Honeywell Incorporated; General Mills, Incorporated; St. Regis Paper Company; 3M Company; and Kimberly-Clark Corporation.

NATIONAL INDUSTRIAL CONFERENCE BOARD, INC., 845 Third Ave., New York, N. Y. 10022
Midwest Office: 120 Oakbrook Mall, Oak Brook, Ill. 60523
THE CONFERENCE BOARD IN CANADA, 615 Dorchester Boulevard West, Montreal 2, Canada
Printed in U. S. A.

Evaluation Manual

For the Improvement of

Elementary Schools

SECTION B.   GENERAL OPERATIONAL PRACTICES AND FACILITIES

Schools are organized and administered so that the education of boys and girls may proceed expeditiously. The nature of the school organization and the type of administrative structure in which the program is carried on will influence markedly the kinds of educational experiences that the school may provide boys and girls.[5]

V.   The Objectives of the School

Since all evaluation of practices and procedures must be done in relation to the objectives of the school, cooperative evaluation of an elementary school program involves an examination of the extent to which the objectives of the school are clearly recognized and stated. Objectives may be stated in many ways. The objectives of the elementary school are usually stated in terms

2. The column headings and their meanings are:
N   Does not apply
M   Missing and Needed
1   Exists to a limited extent
2   Exists to a considerable degree
3   Exists extensively

The Objectives of the School	Evaluation				
	N	M	1	2	3
1. The objectives of the school are formulated cooperatively by pupils, teachers, parents, and administrators.					
2. The objectives of the school are written and in the hands of teachers, administrators, and parents.					
3. The objectives off the school are subject to continuous study and revision.					
4. There is continuous effort to develop understanding of the objectives by: Administrators					
Teachers					
Parents					
5. Physical, social, emotional, spiritual, and mental growth are all emphasized in the statement of objectives.					
6. Individual differences in interest, needs, and abilities of pupils are recognized in the stated objectives.					
7. Democratic living and democratic values are evident in the statement of objectives.					
8. Desirable growth in behavior is included in the statement of objectives.					
Others.					

The Oklahoma State Department of Education

Authors' Note: This example stresses the need for a clear statement of the objectives of the school in order for the study to be meaningful. If the objectives are poorly stated or inaccurate then it's hardly likely that a true study of the school will result.

The Elementary School Guide

ORGANIZATION AND ADMINISTRATION OF THE ELEMENTARY SCHOOL

I. PLANNING AND ORGANIZATION

Statement of Guiding Principles

Unity and continuity in the education of boys and girls are achieved only through cooperative study, planning, action, and evaluation by the entire school staff. The development of the staff into a successful working group is a long-range project, one that is brought about through many and varied experiences in which the members of the staff find group work a satisfying and effective means of achieving results.

Organizing and carrying on faculty meetings, conferences, and workshops and stimulating group effort for curriculum improvement require skill in leadership and cooperation of all concerned. This type of planned, cooperative endeavor is needed:

(a) to develop a worthwhile and well-integrated school program;

(b) to provide opportunities for cooperative thinking, planning, and interchange of ideas;

(c) to develop skill in using group methods and democratic procedures;

(d) to provide a wholesome school atmosphere conducive to well-rounded living and learning.

(e) to keep the curriculum and staff up-to-date.

A. Staff

E S N L 1. The principal has adequate professional training in elementary education and administration.

E S N L 2. The principal has had successful teaching experience in the elementary school.

E S N L 3. Each teacher has been professionally trained for the work which he is doing.

E S N L 4. Before vacancies are filled or new teachers are added, the principal and teachers cooperatively evaluate the school program to determine phases of the program that need strengthening.

E S N L 5. The principal assists in selecting the teachers for his building.

E S N L 6. The school has a satisfactory arrangement by which teachers may visit other schools for professional improvement without loss of pay.

E S N L 7. The school has a satisfactory policy for sick leave with pay.

E S N L 8. There is an overall school plan for substitute teachers to attend professional meetings.

E S N L 9. All teachers are encouraged to join and participate actively in professional organizations.

E S N L 10. There is rotation of opportunity for teachers to participate in educational meetings on county, state, and national levels.

E S N L 11. There is rotation of opportunity for teachers to represent the school on lay committees as speakers for civic and social clubs.

E S N L 12. The school has a plan to have at least one teacher who taught in this school last year serve as a special friend to each new teacher to help him with his professional and personal problems.

State Department of Education
Little Rock, Arkansas

Authors' Note: The organization and administration of the school under study is usually the next item of examination after the purpose, philosophy, and objectives are delineated. The example from Arkansas uses the check list format to point out how the staff is administrated.

A GUIDE FOR THE REVIEW OF A PROGRAM
IN ELEMENTARY EDUCATION

Organization of the School

	Strong Aspect	Needs Improvement
1. There is a clear-cut policy regarding a minimum entrance age for the kindergarten (5 years of age by December is recommended)		
2. Kindergarten groups are usually limited to 20-25 children		
3. Enrolments in grades 1-6 classes usually range from 25-30 children		
4. Children in grades 1-6 attend full-day sessions (at least 5 hours of instruction).		
5. The length of the school day, including travel time, is reasonable for every child		
6. The daily schedule is such that classroom teachers can have large blocks of time for instruction*		
7. There is a well-established promotion policy		
8. In general, childrens' progress is continuous in the elementary school years.		
9. Classes are organized for effective instruction.		
10. Special classes are provided for mentally retarded children		
11. Special provisions are made for physically handicapped pupils		
12. Special provisions are made for gifted pupils.		
13. Teachers use flexible grouping in the classrooms		
14. Social relationships and emotional adjustment are given careful attention in class organizations		
15. The services of special personnel are efficiently utilized by classroom teachers and the principal in guiding pupils		
16. Special provisons are made for children from materially and socially disadvantaged backgrounds		
17. A good system of cumulative records of individual children is carefully kept		

*   The principal should attach sample copies of daily schedules for each grade level.

THE UNIVERSITY OF THE STATE OF NEW YORK
THE STATE EDUCATION DEPARTMENT
COOPERATIVE REVIEW SERVICE
ALBANY, NEW YORK 12224

Authors' Note: The New York State guide is a typical example of statements that can be used to study the organization of an elementary school. The material listed is standard in extent and form.

SELF-STUDY FOR ELEMENTARY SCHOOLS

GUIDELINES FOR WRITING EVALUATIVE CRITERIA

THE ADMINISTRATION

The chief task of educational administration is leadership— the ability to release the creativity, initiative, energy, responsibility, and talents of people. The leader helps others to get things done— things mutually decided upon. Leadership also involves short and long-range planning, the management of resources, the communication of ideas, and the constant evaluation of the progress of the school as a whole toward its goals.

WHAT EVIDENCE IS THERE THAT?

1. Leadership is resulting in high teacher morale.

2. Leadership is resulting in high student morale.

3. Leadership is resulting in widespread teacher initiative and creativity.

4. Leadership is resulting in widespread sharing of new ideas in education.

5. Leadership is developing strong home-school relationships and support.

6. Leadership is developing extensive community involvement, interest, and support with respect to the school, as well as school involvement in the community.

7. Leadership had developed financial procedures and budgetary planning that support a forward-looking educational program.

8. Leadership had created an environment for learning that provides variety, stimulation, and excitement balanced with security and stability.

9. Leadership has developed efficient handling of school routines.

10. Leadership has helped to establish effective relationships with receiving schools.

Published By

The Office of the Gloucester County Superintendent of Schools
County Office of Education, Clayton, New Jersey

Authors' Note: The Gloucester County sample is unique in that it asks for "evidence" of educational leadership in the administration of the school. It is not enough for the response to be that something is done or not; "proof" must be given. A most unusual but pleasantly noteworthy variation.

The Elementary School Guide

III. SUPERVISION   Statement of Guiding Principles

The purpose of supervision is the improvement of teaching and learning. The elementary principal should recognize that his major responsibility is the improvement of curriculum and teaching. He has the opportunity to provide leadership in establishing a good educational program and so developing it from year to year that it becomes increasingly effective in meeting the needs of the children in this changing world.

Equipment and supplies may contribute to better teaching and learning, and through this better teaching and learning the teacher himself may grow in understanding, knowledge, and skill. To render this service, however, equipment and supplies must be carefully selected in terms of their potential contribution to desired goals and then be appropriately used. Frequent evaluation of actual learnings, followed by thoughtful experimentation and then more creative use of materials and resources—this is the process that is most effective in curriculum improvement and teacher growth.

Cooperative planning and evaluation carried on by principal and teachers opens the door for the principal to work with the teachers in solving their problems and finding better ways of teaching. Together they can plan and put into operation a program of in-service education that meets the needs and abilities of all persons concerned.

A. Equipment and Materials: Their Selection and Use

E S N L 1. The school budget provides for the purchase of teaching materials.

E S N L 2. Principal and teachers are alert to available free and inexpensive materials.

E S N L 3. All equipment and materials are selected in terms of their contribution to good living and learning by the children.

E S N L 4. All materials used are in harmony with the philosophy of education held by the staff.

E S N L 5. Equipment and materials are evaluated frequently in terms of meaningful activities which they make possible.

E S N L 6. All materials are appropriate to the maturity and educational levels of the pupils who use them.

E S N L 7. Equipment and supplies are well constructed of appropriate material, designed for repeated, safe use.

E S N L 8. All educational materials used are geared to the interests and experiences of the children concerned.

E S N L 9. Printed and pictorial materials are accurate, authentic, and up-to-date.

E S N L 10. The school has a definite plan for teachers and children to submit requests for specific library books, textbooks, and other teaching materials.

E S N L 11. There is a teacher committee that screens all requests for library books, and, in cooperation with the principal, orders library books. This screening committee includes the school librarian if the school has one.

E S N L 12. There is a teacher committee which screens all requests for equipment and teaching materials other than library books, and in cooperation with the principal, orders equipment and teaching materials.

E S N L 13. The school maintains a card file of all library books.

E S N L 14. The school uses professional help in classifying and organizing the card file or central library.

State Department of Education
Little Rock, Arkansas

continued

Authors' Note: This sample concerns itself with the materials and equipment used by the teachers. In addition, it gives some clues for the evaluation of the selection process of these items.

The Elementary School Guide

III. SUPERVISION

Statement of Guiding Principles

E S N L 15. The school has a definite plan for checking out library books to rooms and individual children.

E S N L 16. The school also has a plan for regular exchange of library books among classrooms where a central library is not provided.

E S N L 17. The school uses other available library facilities—local, state, or regional.

E S N L 18. The school has a plan that makes available to all groups teaching aids that must be used jointly by several groups, such as audio-visual equipment, maps, globes, sewing machine, hot plate, athletic equipment, and encyclopedias.

E S N L 19. Opportunities are provided for teachers to learn to use such curriculum aids as duplicator, tape recorder, filmstrip machine, and movie projector.

E S N L 20. Opportunities are provided for teachers to learn to use various materials or to develop certain skills—for example, to use finger paints, to do manuscript writing, to learn more about teacher-pupil planning, etc.

E S N L 21. Teachers have the skill and knowledge to make effective use of all materials provided.

E S N L 22. Children are given guidance in learning the proper use and care of materials.

E S N L 23. There is convenient storage in each classroom for teaching materials.

E S N L 24. Teaching materials not in current use are removed from the classroom.

E S N L 25. Convenient storage is provided for materials when they are not in use in the class-rooms.

E S N L 26. Provision is made for a central materials center.

E S N L 27. Materials and equipment are kept in repair and in good working condition.

E S N L 28. Teachers study the cause and effect relationship between the use of the teaching materials and the actual learnings of the children.

E S N L 29. There is a school plan that makes available to every group the use of school facilities that must be shared—for example, the auditorium or all purpose room, the health room, the lunch room, the playground, and the gymnasium.

E S N L 30. The school keeps an up-to-date file of resource persons, places, and agencies of interest or service to children.

State Department of Education
Little Rock, Arkansas

ACCREDITATION STANDARDS FOR FLORIDA SCHOOLS

The standards are divided into three levels: *Level 1, Level 2,* and *Level 3.* The meanings of the three levels as used in this document are indicated as follows:

Level 1 Standards: These standards delineate basic indispensable essentials in the school program. They may relate to both what a school has and to the measurable practices employed in implementing the program. The standards naturally tend to be objective and quantitative in nature and include items which are easily appraised. Each Level 1 standard is required to be met in full for a school to be accredited.

Level 2 Standards: These standards are of great importance, but in contrast to Level 1 they are not considered so significant that missing one of them will cause a school to be classified as non-accredited. These requirements are intended to insure functionality of the school as an institution and give scope and effectiveness to its program.

Level 3 Standards: Level 3 standards designate quantities or qualities which make it possible for the school meeting a large number of such standards to achieve added effectiveness in its program. Level 3 standards are designed to define the schools of tomorrow and to offer goals for long-range planning and achievement.

The basic minimum accreditation requirements for each school are: (1) compliance with all of the Level 1 standards, (2) compliance with a stipulated percentage of Level 2 standards, and (3) compliance, very probably, with a smaller percentage of Level 3 standards.

Obviously this system, if properly implemented, will offer excellent possibilities for improving the schools of Florida through establishing an indispensable minimum standard of compliance below which no school may go and be accredited and through offering substantial stimulation to those schools with richer possibilities for achievement. By holding up Level 2 and Level 3 standards as incentives, this system makes it possible to establish desirable long-range goals for improvement.

More Recent Programs

An effort has been made in this edition of the accreditation standards to include the most recent educational developments.

The beginning has been made toward rendering assistance with television education, individual instruction, programed learning, and team teaching. The provisions for experimental programs have been made clearer and, it is hoped, more helpful. This opens the door for the inclusion of other desirable practices.

Organization of Standards

The requirements have been reorganized into four major divisions: (1) The Overall School, (2) The Elementary School, (3) The Junior High School, and (4) The Senior High School. This was designed for the convenience of the local school personnel and the members of the staff of the State Department of Education in administering the program. The principals will be required to fill out only the part relating to the overall school and those sections appropriate to the organization of the reporting school.

The Divisional System

The divisional system in the Accreditation Standards is the same as that used in all of the Regulations of the State Board of Education. The accreditation standards have been arranged so that content relating to a given subject may be identified throughout the document. In qualifications of personnel, for example, Sections 563, 573, 583, 593 are used. It will be observed that the same digit comes before the period whether the section number appears in the overall school, the elementary school, the junior high school, or the senior high school. A like arrangement has been made for the other major divisions. In the completed document the Standards will carry the identifying number *130* which has been assigned to all Regulations of the State Board of Education.

Accreditation Classifications

The present commitment provides for four possible accreditation classifications: *Non-Accredited, Accredited, Advanced Accredited,* and *Superior Accredited.* The accredited classifications will be derived from meeting all Level 1 standards plus graduated percentages of Level 2 standards and Level 3 standards for each classification. To provide for continuous stimulation the requirements for compliance with Level 2 and Level 3 standards will be increased as the schools of Florida progress. Similar bases are laid for publishing accreditation classifications in *The Florida*

STATE DEPARTMENT OF EDUCATION
Tallahassee, Florida

Authors' Note: Some states are classifying schools, or grading them in terms of quality, or of their ability to meet certain standards. The Florida example sets three standards and three levels of accreditation classifications.

II. BASIC DATA REGARDING THE COMMUNITY
A. POPULATION DATA FOR THE SCHOOL COMMUNITY (See "Definitions" on page 18)

Year to which information applies: 19

Describe the area included within your community:

1. Total population this year (census date _____)   _____

2. Total population last census (census date _____)   _____

3. Number of youth of secondary school age in the community   _____

4. Number of secondary schools of all types in this community and enrollment:

	NO. OF SCHOOLS	TOTAL ENROLLMENT
Public	_____	_____
Church-related	_____	_____
Nonpublic, non–church-related	_____	_____
Total	_____	_____

5. Enrollment in this school   _____

B. OCCUPATIONAL STATUS OF ADULTS

Describe briefly the general character of employment of adults in the community. If the school is *publicly* supported, recent census data of the supporting district may be satisfactory. If the school is *nonpublic*, a summary of occupations of parents of present students will be helpful.

C. EDUCATIONAL STATUS OF ADULTS

Describe, in general, the extent of the formal education of parents and other adults in the community. If recent census reports are not available, an estimate should be made by those who know the community well.

D. ECONOMIC CLIMATE

Explain any changes in the economic development of the community within the past ten years.

EVALUATIVE CRITERIA
Fourth Edition

continued

Authors' Note: It is always helpful if certain data is collected which will assist the evaluation by providing the necessary background material for review. Community data, the extent and nature of the course offerings, and student ability are some of the common material that is collected. The sample is from the secondary schools but can be easily adapted for the elementary school.

B. STUDENT ABILITY

1. Academic ability

a) If records of intelligence or academic ability tests are available, give number of students in each of the following IQ or percentile ranges. If the school does not have data suitable for this table, give equivalent distribution either in this form, revised as necessary, or on a separate sheet. If neither request can be met, describe briefly the general academic ability of students. If the school is ungraded, or for other reasons the organization does not lend itself to this table, modify or replace it so that the school is accurately described.

RANGE*		SEVENTH GRADE	EIGHTH GRADE	NINTH GRADE	TENTH GRADE	ELEVENTH GRADE	TWELFTH GRADE	TOTAL	
I Q	National Percentile							Number	Percent
Over 124	Over 94								
117–124	85–94								
109–116	70–84								
92–108	31–69								
84– 91	16–30								
76– 83	6–15								
Below 76	Below 6								
Total									

* A school should feel free to modify these intervals to agree with distributions previously made. Indicate which column is being used by circling "IQ" or "National Percentile."

b) What test or tests were used in determining these data?

c) When were the tests given?

2. What test data, other than academic ability, are available that describe the abilities of students?

3. Describe how test data are used to identify abilities of students and to plan their educational programs.

4. List and describe any long-range studies carried on by the school that relate to student abilities.

EVALUATIVE CRITERIA
Fourth Edition

by National Study of Secondary School Evaluation, *1785 Massachusetts Avenue, N.W., Washington, D.C. 20036. All rights reserved. No part of this material may be reproduced in any form without prior written permission of the publisher.*

continued

B. ORGANIZATION OF OFFERINGS—Continued

Supplementary Data—Continued

3. List the fields of study or courses for which the following are available:

a) Ability-grouped *sequences*

_____

_____

_____

b) Remedial programs

_____

_____

_____

c) Programs for the academically talented
   (1) Advanced placement

_____

_____

_____

   (2) Honors courses

_____

_____

_____

   (3) Advanced seminars

_____

_____

d) Ungraded classes

_____

_____

_____

e) Summer school

_____

_____

_____

f) Television

_____

_____

_____

g) Programed materials

_____

_____

_____

h) Teacher aides

_____

_____

i) Departmental learning laboratories

_____

_____

_____

j) Correspondence study

_____

_____

_____

k) Team teaching

_____

_____

_____

l) Large-group arrangement

_____

_____

_____

EVALUATIVE CRITERIA
Fourth Edition

Standards
for
Accrediting
Elementary
Schools
in Virginia

Library Services

Library services shall be provided in each school. Services of a qualified librarian shall be provided as follows:

—part time for schools with less than twelve (12) regular classroom teachers.

—full time for schools with twelve (12) or more regular classroom teachers.

Membership

1. The average membership in kindergarten classrooms shall not exceed twenty (20) children per teacher, and membership in an individual kindergarten classroom shall not exceed twenty-five (25) children per teacher.

2. The average membership in elementary classrooms (grades 1-7) shall not exceed thirty (30) children per teacher, and membership for an individual classroom shall not exceed thirty-five (35) children per teacher.

3. Special education services shall be available to each school. Class size for these special education groups shall be:

—Mentally Retarded

Educable —membership not to exceed sixteen (16) children per teacher

Trainable—membership not to exceed twelve (12) children per teacher

—Emotionally Disturbed (when grouped for classroom instruction)

Primary   —membership not to exceed eight (8) children per teacher

Elementary—membership not to exceed twelve (12) children per teacher

Age of School Entrance

1. The local school board may admit persons who have reached their fifth (5) birthday on or before September thirtieth (30) of any year to the kindergarten. (Virginia School Laws, Section 22-218.2)

2. The local school board shall admit persons who have reached their sixth (6) birthday on or before September thirtieth (30) of any year to the primary grades. (Virginia School Law, Section 22-218)

Length of School Year

The length of the regular school session shall be for a period of not less than 180 teaching days. Local school boards are encouraged to use the additional time provided in teacher contracts for curriculum development and professional conferences.

Length of School Day

The length of the regular school day shall not be less than five (5) nor more than six and one-half (6½) hours, exclusive of time for the mid-day intermission, with the exception that a minimum day of five (5) hours for the kindergarten may include the mid-day intermission.

ELEMENTARY EDUCATION SERVICE
STATE DEPARTMENT OF EDUCATION
RICHMOND, VIRGINIA 23216

Secretarial Services

1. Each school with an enrollment of 300 or more shall have a full-time secretary.

Authors' Note: In an effort to upgrade education in some states the State Department of Education publishes material for local guidance and direction. This will give the local school a standard to work towards that is not suspect because it is home-grown. In the Virginia example the local schools are also given policy guidelines for review and inclusion in the local situation.

Standards
of
Mississippi
Accrediting
Commission

IV. In-Service Education

     The superintendent shall provide a continuous in-service education program regardless of the education of faculty members.

     An in-service program should include the following:

A. A program for the study and the improvement of instruction on such topics as methods of teaching, curriculum, program and course objectives, evaluations, child growth and development, and similar topics.

B. The accessibility for teachers and staff of professional books magazines, bulletins, and other professional materials.

C. Opportunities for visits to other schools and observation of their work.

D. Leaves of absence for attendance at colleges and universities for both undergraduate and graduate study.

E. Utilization of educational leadership through interchange of competent teachers from all levels of education.

Standards For Accrediting Public And Private Elementary And Secondary Schools

---

    Authors' Note: One of the most neglected areas in the evaluation process is the in-service program and the analysis of that program. Only a few states list this item as a firm recommendation and state that it will be a significant part of the evaluation criteria.

Instructional Program
and Materials

EVALUATING AND IMPROVING
Nebraska Elementary Schools

PROGRAM OF STUDIES—SCOPE AND ORGANIZATION

The scope of all the learning experience which a child has in school under the supervision of his teachers comprises what is commonly known as the curriculum of that school. A wholesome curriculum must provide for the development of the basic skills of reading, writing, spelling, speaking, listening and arithmetic. In addition, it must guide the child in making such use of these skills as will contribute most to his becoming a responsible and contributing member of society. A sound curriculum must also help the child develop habits, appreciations, attitudes and understandings needed for living usefully and happily in our democracy.

The school's daily program of studies is the formal organization of the curriculum to provide daily learning experiences which best meet the needs of the children. The well-planned program is always sufficiently flexible to meet the changing needs and conditions.

Level I	Level II	Level III	Level IV	Level V	Needs Indicated for Our Program
CURRICULUM A. Curriculum consists of teaching all children the same facts and skills and presenting them as more or less isolated aspects of learning. There is no selection of the facts and skills to help improve the particular group.	Curriculum consists of teaching all children the same facts and skills, but some choice is made of facts and skills which the pupils may need in the future.	Curriculum consists of teaching all children the same facts, skills, and habits, but some selection is made of those which will help the children in their present-day living.	Curriculum consists of the same experiences for all children in the development of knowledges, skills, habits, and understandings, but the experiences selected are those which will help the group, both in their present living and in their future life.	Curriculum consists of experiences which will help develop habits, knowledges, understandings, ideals, attitudes and skills for present and future living in a democracy. These experiences are selected according to the needs, abilities, and interests, not only of the group but of each child.	

State of Nebraska

Dept. of Education

Lincoln, Nebraska

Authors' Note: There are five levels of curriculum programs in this Nebraska example. It may assist the evaluation process if standards are available for comparison to the local situation.

MINIMUM STANDARDS FOR PUBLIC SCHOOLS

(3) Staff Adequacy:

(a) Daily Class Load:

1. In elementary schools, the average class load within a school in grades one, two, and three is not to exceed a maximum of 25 pupils ADM . The class load average within a school in grades four, five, six, seven, and eight is not to exceed a maximum of 30 pupils. The class load for a teacher assigned to teach three or more grades is not to exceed a maximum of 20 students ADM. The class load for a teacher assigned to teach two grades is not to exceed a maximum of 25 students. When the class loads are at or over the maximum, consideration shall be given for district-wide supervisory assistance and for use of teacher aides in the classroom.

> Adopted by the State Board of
> Education September 14, 1966,
> Issued by the Department of
> Education ***
> Superintendent of Public Instruction
> Salem, Oregon 97310

Authors' Note: Class load is one of the most difficult areas for the faculty and administration to consider. This is particularly true where the local teachers are in teacher associations that are well organized. Some states set standards; others only issue recommendations.

Handbook

for

Classification

and

Accreditation

Standards For Elementary Schools

4. Teaching Load

Class AAA

At least one teacher shall be provided for each grade taught (including kindergarten) except where students from more than one grade level are grouped in a classroom unit to improve instruction. Elementary teachers shall be scheduled at least forty minutes of planning time within the six-hour school day. Teacher aides should be provided to relieve teachers of nonprofessional tasks.

Sufficient classroom teachers shall be provided to keep the classroom teacher-pupil ratio at 1 to 30 or fewer. Individual classrooms with more than 30 students will be considered excessive. In cooperative teaching projects (such as team teaching) an individual classroom teacher may instruct more than 30 students part of the time, but the average classroom teacher load shall not exceed one classroom teacher to 30 students.

Classes for performing groups in vocal and instrumental music and physical education may enroll more than 30 pupils.

The supervisor or subject matter specialist (spending one-half time or more supervising teachers) load shall be on the basis of one full-time supervisor to seventy teachers. The teaching specialist load shall be on the basis of one full-time teaching specialist to 600 students.

The primary purpose of teacher aides is to enable the teacher to improve the quality of instruction, and aides should be used in addition to the standards for professional personnel.

In some districts, a classroom shortage may make it impossible to maintain all individual classroom enrollments in accordance with the standards. Where it is deemed necessary, the use of a teacher assistant in individual classrooms exceeding the enrollment standard may be considered as a way of meeting the classroom enrollment standard. The individual classroom enrollment may be increased by 10 students for any period that a teacher assistant assists the classroom teacher full time. A teacher with a half-time teacher assistant could be assigned an additional 5 students or a teacher with a full-time teacher assistant could be assigned an additional 10 students.

Department of Education
State of Missouri

Authors' Note: The state of Missouri sets limits on class loads and indicates the procedure if the maximums are surpassed. The teacher aide suggestions are becoming common in many states and in many teacher negotiated contracts.

CRITERIA FOR CLASS SIZE
AND SPECIALISTS

INTRODUCTION

What is the best class size for elementary
and secondary schools remains largely un-
answered. Contemporary research indicates
that no argument can be made for any arbitrary, common optimum class size. Desirable class size is determined by local
conditions, the kind of education desired
and the abilities of the teachers. Although research has produced no specific
answers to the question of desirable class
size, the weight of contemporary evidence
lies in small classes.

Grade Level: **KINDERGARTEN**

Standards recommended by:

National Commission on
Teacher Education and
Professional Standards, NEA 20

National Education
Association .... 25 max.

New Jersey State
Department of Education .... 25 max.

Association of Childhood
Education, International 25

Association for Supervision
and Curriculum Development, NEA... 25

Department of Elementary-
Kindergarten-Nursery Edu-
cation, NEA-1964 Resolution 25

Association of Classroom
Teachers, NEA 25-30

Grade Level: **ELEMENTARY**

Standards recommended by:

Association for Supervision
and Curriculum Development, NEA... 25 max.

National Education
Association .... 25 max.

Association of Childhood
Education, International 25

Department of Elementary-
Kindergarten-Nursery Edu-
cation, NEA 25

National Commission on
Teacher Education and
Professional Standards, NEA 25

Association of Classroom
Teachers, NEA 25-30

Southern Association of
Colleges and Schools 30

Grade Level: **HIGH SCHOOL**

Standards recommended by:

Association for Supervision
and Curriculum Development, NEA... 25 max.

National Commission on
Teacher Education and
Professional Standards, NEA....... 25

North Central Association
of Colleges and
Secondary Schools 27

Association of Classroom
Teachers, NEA.................... 25-30

Commission on Secondary
Schools of N. W. Association
of Secondary and Higher
Education 25-30

SPECIAL EDUCATION REQUIREMENTS

From the Rules and Regulations of the New Jersey
State Board of Education pertaining to Special
Education - Chapter 29 of New Jersey Public Laws
of 1966 .....

Class size and grouping shall be appropri-
ated to the disability and need of the child
involved. In the following categories or
subcategories, the maximum enrollment shall
not exceed:

Multiple Handicapped	8
General Orthopedic	15
Visually Handicapped	8
Auditory Handicapped	8
Chronically Ill	20
Educable —	15
Trainable	10
Emotionally Disturbed	8
Neurologically Impaired —	8
Perceptually Impaired	12
Socially Maladjusted	12
Communication Handicapped	10

NEW JERSEY EDUCATION ASSOCIATION
180 West State Street, Trenton, N. J. 08608

Authors' Note: State Teacher Associations have been in the forefront of working towards class
size standards. In this example the Association buttresses its suggestions with the standards of other
professional groups.

MULTI-AGE GROUPING:

In some schools, extracurricular activities contribute to a natural mixing of ages. Let's look at some actual situations we have observed in schools which involve multi-age grouping and examine the values that emerge.

Situation: The elementary school safety council we visited was composed of representatives from every class. The council had scheduled a series of meetings to study school accidents. The older children made charts to illustrate unsafe practices. The younger children coined slogans to go with the charts. Later, all the children in the council together put on a special assembly program to help stop the spread of accidents. The older children showed slides of dangerous activities and explained how these activities could be made accident-proof. Younger children recited original safety poems. The youngest showed safety charts and explained their slogans.

Values: Are there values to children when they study common problems? Isn't this a realistic experience for children, who, as adults, will have to work cooperatively with others? If so, then why do we, in America, have such a cleavage of age groups, such a generation gap, when collaboration of efforts and ideas from young and old would unify attitudes and help to eliminate antagonisms? Surely problems of our society must be attacked by combining the thinking of multi-age groups, rather than by separating and pitting one against the other. Safety, health, crime, smog, littering are problems contributed to by all age groups and must be attacked by multi-aged thinking. Schools, by grade and age segregation, give little opportunity for the interaction of children of many ages and as a result perpetuate a pecking-order based on age.

Situation: The elementary school council — also composed of representatives from every class — met to consider the effect of such

things as manners in the cafeteria, nutrition, and school safety on the school. Afterwards, each representative went back to his classroom to lead a discussion. At the next council meeting which we attended each representative reported the suggestions of his classmates on how undesirable behavior could be lessened. These suggested rules from each grade became school-wide policy.

Values: Do children in multi-age groups experience more cooperation than competition? Is it possible that when the age range is narrowed, more competitive behavior occurs?

Situation: In one school where two lunch periods were required, the staff decided not to separate the younger and older children during lunch. After mixing older children with younger ones in each lunch period, a great many examples of cooperation, helpfulness, instruction, and pleasant interaction were observed by the committee.

Values: Does multi-age grouping create a social environment in which more opportunities arise for certain desired kinds of social behavior to occur? Does this type of situation affect the attitudes of children toward social behavior appropriate for various ages?

Situation: Several members of the Service Corps (9- to 11-year-old children) were returning from the playground of the five- and six-year-olds where they had been teaching little ones to play jacks, jump rope, bat balls, and learn similar skills. Some of their comments we overheard follow: "Tommy really is trying to hit the ball. He won't give up trying." "Sometimes the boys and girls change the rules of the game, but when they find out their rules don't work, they go back to the 'real rules.'" "Each day I get more girls to learn to jump rope. They watch and help each other." "You know, I like teaching them. I want to be a teacher when I grow up."

Values: Is there opportunity for youngsters to gain more insight into human striving, conniving, initiating, imitating when they are involved

DEPARTMENT OF ELEMENTARY-KINDERGARTEN-NURSERY EDUCATION
NATIONAL EDUCATION ASSOCIATION OF THE UNITED STATES

Authors' Note: It is most difficult to find material that is specifically for the multi-age school. The sample from the National Education Association illustrates a process and situation that can be used by the local group in assessing this type of organization. This situation-value process is not limited to schools that are organized non-traditionally. It is useful for any school regardless of organization.

STANFORD ACHIEVEMENT TEST

Ranking on National Norms, Rectified Grade Equivalents by I.Q. and Actual Grade

Equivalents:

	Grade 5		Grade 6	
	Rectified G.E. by I.Q. Level	Actual B.H.* G.E.**	Rectified G.E. by I.Q. Level	Actual B.H.* G.E.**
Word Meaning	6.3	7.2	7.6	8.6
Paragraph Meaning	6.5	7.2	7.8	8.6
Spelling	6.3	6.8	7.4	8.2
Language	6.6	7.5	7.8	9.0
Arithmetic Comprehensive	6.1	6.9	7.7	9.3
Arithmetic Concepts	6.0	6.9	7.3	9.3
Arithmetic Applications	6.4	6.9	7.7	9.3
Social Studies	6.4	7.7	7.7	9.6
Science	6.3	7.2	7.5	8.8

* Byram Hills
** Grade Equivalent

Key: The Rectified Grade Equivalent column indicates the level of achievement which Byram Hills students are expected to attain above the national level, taking into consideration their high level of ability. Example: The National Norm for Grade 5 is 5.9 (5th year, ninth month). Byram Hills Rectified Norm in word meaning would be 6.3. In actuality the Byram Hills achieved Grade Equivalent was 7.2. In other words, our students scored nine months higher than students of similar mental ability, and 1 year three months higher than randomly selected students throughout the nation.

BYRAM HILLS SCHOOL DISTRICT
EUGENE J. BRADFORD, DISTRICT PRINCIPAL
ARMONK, NEW YORK

Authors' Note: A truly unique exhibit is this next example. It is one of the few, if not the only school district, that made allowances for the unique ability of the students in the interpretation of test results. Most schools simply compare themselves to a national or regional standard and do not make allowances for the particular nature of the student body.

A DECADE OF DECISION 1952-1962

Ten-Year Report

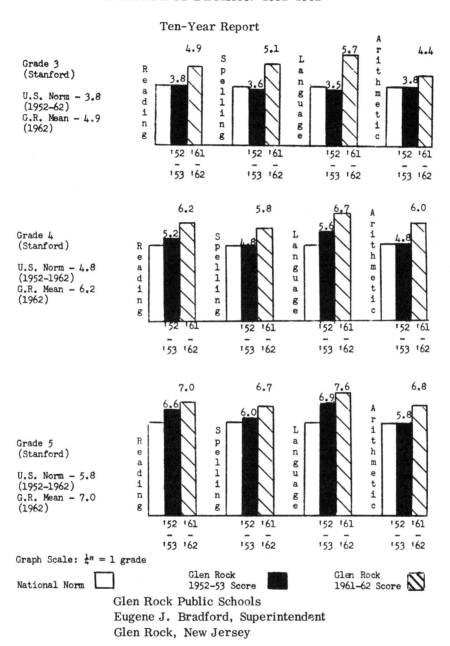

Grade 3
(Stanford)

U.S. Norm – 3.8
(1952-62)
G.R. Mean – 4.9
(1962)

Grade 4
(Stanford)

U.S. Norm – 4.8
(1952-1962)
G.R. Mean – 6.2
(1962)

Grade 5
(Stanford)

U.S. Norm – 5.8
(1952-1962)
G.R. Mean – 7.0
(1962)

Graph Scale: ¼" = 1 grade

National Norm ☐   Glen Rock
1952-53 Score ■   Glen Rock
1961-62 Score ⧄

Glen Rock Public Schools
Eugene J. Bradford, Superintendent
Glen Rock, New Jersey

Authors' Note: It is most helpful to the board of education if long-termed results can be proven. It can be used to prove that increased achievements are due to any variable that can be used, such as more or newer textbooks, smaller class size, better qualified teachers. However, the long term results must first be gathered.

D. METHODS OF EVALUATION

Checklist

1. Evaluating and recording class and individual accomplishment are an integral part of the teaching-learning activities.   na 1 2 3 4
2. Evaluation is pursued through oral and written, subjective and objective means.   na 1 2 3 4
3. Students participate in the evaluation of their own progress.   na 1 2 3 4
4. Consistent effort is made through the use of testing devices to determine the abilities of all students in reading, writing, speaking, and listening.   na 1 2 3 4
5. Evaluation of students' use of language is based on observation by the teacher as well as on results of standardized tests.   na 1 2 3 4
6. Evaluation is used to identify students needing remedial instruction.   na 1 2 3 4
7. Objective evidence is obtained of the reading interests of students.   na 1 2 3 4

8. Cumulative records are kept of students' reading.   na 1 2 3 4
9. In evaluating speaking and writing, emphasis is given to content, organization, quality of thought, and style as well as to mechanics.   na 1 2 3 4
10. Ability to work in groups is evaluated.   na 1 2 3 4
11. Careful checks are made to determine comprehension of independent reading.   na 1 2 3 4
12. Both teachers and students recognize that tests are used to reveal strengths and to suggest areas for further study.   na 1 2 3 4
13. Teachers use evaluation results as one index of their own teaching effectiveness and plan their instruction accordingly.   na 1 2 3 4
14.   na 1 2 3 4

Supplementary Data

1. Describe the achievement testing program in English.

2. Show how this program is used to evaluate:
   a) Strengths, weaknesses, and yearly growth of individual students.
   b) Class achievement on national or other norms.
   c) Class weaknesses.

Evaluations

a) *How adequate are the evaluation procedures in English?*   na 1 2 3 4
b) *How well do teachers use evaluation results in analyzing the effectiveness of their teaching?*   na 1 2 3 4
c) *To what extent do evaluation procedures identify students of unusual promise in the field of English?*   na 1 2 3 4
d) *To what extent do evaluation procedures identify students with unusual needs in the field of English?*   na 1 2 3 4

Comments

Authors' Note: Pupil evaluation is almost as much of a problem as teacher evaluation. Indeed many of the same discussions could be used for either area. This example from the secondary school is most easily adapted for the elementary school.

The Elementary School Guide

B. Evaluation

E S N L   1. Principal, teachers, children, and parents cooperatively evaluate activities, learnings, and needs of the school frequently throughout the year.

E S N L   2. These evaluations are recorded and are used as the basis for developing future policies and plans.

E S N L   3. Various materials and techniques are used in evaluating individual learnings and the effectiveness of different ways of teaching—observation, group planning and evaluating, anecdotal records of child behavior, informal testing, standardized tests, sample of work, parent-teacher conferences, parent-child conferences, action research, etc.

E S N L   4. All phases of the growth or development of each child are carefully considered and evaluated.

E S N L   5. All phases of the school program are evaluated.

E S N L   6. Each child's growth and achievement are evaluated in terms of his own progress, in relation to his interests, experiences, abilities, efforts, needs, and stage of development, not by comparing him with other children or with age or grade norms.

E S N L   7. Standardized intelligence and/or achievement tests are used for diagnosis and guidance, not solely for grouping or grading children or for evaluating teachers.

E S N L   8. All test scores are considered personal and confidential.

E S N L   9. It is the policy of the school not to disclose to parents the I.Q. scores of their children.

E S N L 10. **The Guide** is studied and discussed by the professional staff and is used as a means for cooperative evaluation and school improvement.

E S N L 11. Evaluation of teacher-effectiveness is made by the teacher himself and jointly by teacher and principal or by teacher, principal, and supervisor.

State Department of Education
Little Rock, Arkansas

Authors' Note: Evaluation in general is a current, frequent topic of concern to all levels of the public education sector. The national government, state departments, professional organizations, and as always the local school districts, find this area most relevant and tend to apply the concept of evaluation to all areas of the school district. This includes the business function, the learning process, the teaching procedure.

LANGUAGE ARTS PROGRESS REPORT

PUPIL _____ SCHOOL _____ TEACHER _____ CONFERENCE DATES _____

LANGUAGE ARTS AREAS	LEVEL A	LEVEL B	LEVEL C	LEVEL D	LEVEL E	LEVEL F	LEVEL G
AUDITORY DISCRIMINATION	Recognizes: Sounds, Rhyming words	Hears: Consonants in various positions in words, consonant combinations. Matches sounds to symbols	Hears consonant combinations. Identifies sounds in words. Distinguishes vowel sounds	Hears: Differences between single consonants and blends, parts in compound words	Hears: Vowel digraphs, phonograms, "r" influenced words, contractions, triple blends	Hears: Vowel digraphs, Schwa sound, Syllables	Hears: Multi-syllables in words, accent
VISUAL DISCRIMINATION	Matches. Recognizes likenesses and differences. Moves eyes from left to right. Identifies objects	Identifies and matches: Upper and lower case letters, color words	Discriminates between similar symbols. Recognizes: Common components, plural endings	Recognizes: Vowels, compound words, prefixes, blends. *common components. *Makes transition to T.O.	Recognizes: Vowel digraphs, "r" influenced words, word parts, contractions, triple blends, prefixes and suffixes	Recognizes: Parts of words, syllable patterns	Recognizes: Common components of words, syllables
LISTENING	Knows sounds. Reacts to games and stories. Follows simple directions	Gives reasons for reactions to stories, recordings. Follows 2-step directions	Replies and reacts to questions. Follows 3-step directions. Forms visual images	Comments to others. Gets meaning from context or voice. Reacts to speaker. Retells main ideas	Follows 4-step directions. Respects ideas of others. Answers questions. Retells story in sequence	Follows 5-step directions. Shows adequate concentration. Listens with responsibility for facts, ideas, etc.	Adapts skill to purpose. Recognizes: Sound pattern, important ideas
ORAL EXPRESSION	Avoids immature speech. Organizes ideas. Enjoys and participates in speaking activities	Retells, in sequence, short stories heard	Retells, in sequence, stories heard and read	Shares and interprets information. Role plays in small groups. Applies acceptable speaking standards	Uses acceptable speaking standards. Recounts in order. Shows vocabulary growth. Participates in oral activities	Selects topics and plans talks. Gives book reports from simple notes. Develops ideas and keeps to subject. Respects opinions of others	Keeps interest of audience. Speaks in complete, concise sentences. Keeps talks within a time limit. Chooses variety of sentence beginnings. Includes necessary and correct facts in proper sequence. Gives report which develops one main incident or character
MOTOR SKILLS AND HANDWRITING	Traces, copies and draws basic shapes. Handles materials properly. Recognizes writing as a form. Copies name correctly	Writes: Names, letters, *ITA characters, *words	Writes: Short words, simple sentences, *stories. Copies: Simple sentences, Short stories	Attempts to write legibly	Writes neatly and legibly. Slants and spaces letters and words properly and uniformly	Makes clear distinction between capital and lower case letters	Applies standards for good writing to daily classroom and homework assignments
WORD ANALYSIS		Uses picture and letter clues to identify words	Matches pictures and beginning sounds. *Uses consonant clues to identify words. *Blends symbols to form new words	Uses phonics to attack words. Sounds compound words	Uses: Vowel digraphs "r" influenced vowels. Sounds word parts. Attacks words independently	Uses schwa sound. Divides words into syllables. Accents words	Unlocks multi-syllable words. Applies rules of accenting. Changes meaning through use of prefixes and suffixes
WORD STUDY	Develops vocabulary through listening and speaking	Displays curiosity about words	Uses picture dictionary. Identifies similar words quickly. Recognizes words rapidly. Understands meanings of words	Identifies and uses comparison words. Understands some antonyms and synonyms	Makes personal dictionary. Selects words precisely. Understands some multi-meaning words	Uses exact descriptive words. Understands homonyms. Gets meaning from contextual clues. Builds words from common components	Understands syllabication. Builds words from its regular components. Substitutes descriptive words for dull, neutral words
ORAL READING			Reads in phrases. Reads with expression. Answers questions	Understands material read. Re-reads for information. Recalls details. Observes punctuation. Understands 's and quotation marks	Reads in thought units. Enunciates clearly	Reads expressively poetry and parts in plays. Adapts voice to reading situation	Interprets meaning through punctuation. Reads fluently. Dramatizes characters in play
SILENT READING AND COMPREHENSION	Arranges pictures in sequence	Interprets pictures	Thinks critically about pictures. Understands and reacts to stories. Reads to answer specific questions	Rereads to locate information. Follows written directions. Reads in sequence. Expresses opinion about materials read	Distinguishes between fact and fiction. Chooses correct meaning from context	Reads for detail. Interprets figures of speech. Understands meaning of different type. Understands informative material. Notes sequence.	Understands pattern of material. Selects main ideas. Understands sequence of time, place and events. Reads critically
WRITTEN EXPRESSION		*Writes simple sentences	*Writes short stories	Composes simple sentences. Develops simple topic. Creates own stories	Distinguishes between statement and question. Places sentences in logical order. Identifies sentences which do not belong. Writes original stories and poems. Participates in group letter writing	Writes complete sentences and questions. Develops proper paragraph. Writes creatively. Knows parts of letter. Applies correct standards for writing letters, notes and reports	Understands sentence structure. Uses more complex sentences. Writes in a variety of forms. Writes acceptable reports from outlines
MECHANICS				Punctuates simple sentences	Capitalizes proper nouns. Punctuates statements correctly. Uses comma in date. Uses irregular verbs correctly. Uses subjects and verbs that agree	Applies basic rules of capitalization and punctuation. Recognizes and uses parts of speech in building sentences	Applies more complex rules for punctuation, capitalization and usage
SPELLING				Understands concept of spelling. Spells phonetic words correctly	Spells weekly unit words correctly. Shows positive carry over in written work. Uses simple dictionary to confirm spelling	Spells abbreviations and contractions. Spells homonyms at level. Shows increasing ability to spell words not previously learned	Shows mastery. Spells plurals and possessives. Identifies change in root before adding suffix. Takes dictation
STUDY SKILLS	Classifies shapes	Classifies objects and pictures	Classifies objects and pictures in several categories	Classifies words. Keeps simple records	Arranges words in alphabetical order by first letter. Selects titles for stories. Uses table of contents	Alphabetizes by first 2 letters. Begins steps in outlining. Uses parts of books	Uses reference skills. Alphabetizes by first 3 letters. Uses outlining skills. Knows techniques for correct informational reading
INTEREST AND APPRECIATION	Enjoys library	Shows interest in books. Works independently. Completes tasks on time	Pays attention. Creates stories. Evaluates endings. Shares reading experiences	Reads in spare time	Makes use of library	Reads voluntarily. Discusses books read with others. Reads variety of material. Appreciates vivid language	Enjoys reading for information and recreation. Appreciates different forms of literature. Reads widely. Motivates self voluntarily

continued

Authors' Note: The reporting systems for pupil progress are having a thorough review in all parts of the country and by all levels of the educational scene from the elementary school to the

THE MONTCLAIR PUBLIC SCHOOLS, MONTCLAIR, NEW JERSEY
MATHEMATICS PROGRESS REPORT

PUPIL _____ SCHOOL _____ TEACHER _____ CONFERENCE DATES _____

MATH AREAS	LEVEL A	LEVEL B	LEVEL C	LEVEL D	LEVEL E	LEVEL F	LEVEL G	LEVEL H	LEVEL I	LEVEL J
NUMERATION	Recognizes: size, patterns, numerals 0-12. Identifies numbers 0-12, cardinals 0-12, ordinals 1st-5th. Compares sets according to value. Matches sets one-to-one	Uses symbols (>, <) to 100. Identifies: sets to 100, positional relations, odd & even numbers, ordinals to 12th, words as number names. Counts, writes numerals to 12. Counts, writes numbers before, after, between. Skip counts by 5's, 10's	Uses symbols (>, <, =) to 200. Orders ordinals to 20th, words as number names. Counts, writes numerals. Skip counts by 2's, 5's	Uses symbols (>, <, =) to 500. Identifies: ordinals to 50th, words as number names. Counts, writes numerals	Identifies words as number names to 1000. Counts, writes numerals	Identifies words as number names to 10,000. Counts, writes numerals. Skip counts by 3's, 4's	Identifies words as number names, 100,000 -1,000,000	Rounds numbers to nearest designated value		
PLACE VALUE		Identifies: sets of 10 to 100, meaning of symbol "10" numeral for the number, place value of tens ones. Uses: expanded notation, symbols (>, <)	Identifies place value to 200. Uses: expanded notation, symbols (>, <)	Identifies place value to 500. Uses: expanded notation, symbols (>, <)	Identifies place value to 1000. Uses: expanded notation, symbols (>, <)	Identifies place value to 10,000. Regroups in expanded notation through hundreds	Identifies place value to 100,000 and 1,000,000			
ADDITION and SUBTRACTION		Identifies: number in pictured set & number in combined sets, number of a set & various subsets, numerals 0-12. Identifies sums & differences thru 12, subtraction as an inverse operation. Uses: equations, commutative & vertical notation, zero principles	Identifies sums & differences through 18. Checks addition & subtraction. Uses symbols (>, <) in compare equations. Finds missing addends. Adds & subtracts through 99 (no regrouping). Solves word problems (no regrouping)	Adds & subtracts through hundreds (regrouping). Solves word problems (regrouping)	Adds & subtracts through thousands (regrouping). Adds single digits in equations & vertical notation. Uses associative principle	Adds columns (regrouping). Solves word problems (regrouping)				
MULTIPLICATION and DIVISION				Identifies: equivalent sets & states total, total set & divides into equal subsets	Identifies: symbols X, ÷, principles, missing factors & products. Uses terms: factor, times, product, divided by. Multiplies & divides through 5 x 5. Solves word problems	Identifies: Mult. as repeated addition, div. as repeated subt. symbol. Uses terms: divisor, dividend, quotient, divided. Uses vertical notation. Multiplies & divides: through 9 x 9, with one-digit multiplier and divisor (no regrouping)	Uses term "remainder". Multiplies & divides: with one- and two-digit multipliers and divisors (regrouping). Uses mult. & div algorithm. Checks multiplication & division. Solves word problems	Multiplies & divides with two or more digit multipliers & divisors. Solves word problems	Estimates quotients	
COMBINATION of PROCESSES					Identifies missing symbols (+, -, X, ÷). Solves equations	Identifies: symbols (>, <, =). Solves: problems (no regrouping), word problems	Solves: problems (regrouping), word problems	Solves word problems		
FRACTIONS and DECIMALS		Identifies: wholes halves thirds fourths. Uses word names	Identifies: numerals 1/2, 1/3, 1/4, meaning of fractions. Solves word problems	Identifies: numerals 1/5, 2/3, 3/4, numerator & denominator	Identifies fractions thru tenths. Solves word problems	Identifies: common fractions, equivalent fractions. Uses: symbols (>, <, =). Adds like fractions to make a whole. Orders sets of fractional numbers	Identifies: equivalent fractions in lower & higher terms, whole numbers as fractions, improper & mixed numerals, fractional parts of whole numbers with whole number answers	Adds & subtracts: like fractions, mixed fractions. Writes fractions as decimals with tenths, hundredths. Solves word problems	Adds & subtracts: unlike fractions, mixed fractions. Writes fractions as decimals with thousandths. Identifies place value of decimals	Multiplies fractions. Divides fractions. Adds decimals. Subtracts decimals. Solves word problems
MONEY	Recognizes: penny nickel dime	Identifies: numerical value of penny, nickel, dime, coin symbol (¢). Counts pennies	Identifies: numerical value of a dime, coin collections to 99¢. Solves word problems	Identifies: numerical value of quarter, half dollar, symbols—decimal point (.), dollar sign ($), symbols (>, <, =). Skip counts	Identifies: numerical value of bills. Makes change. Solves word problems	Adds dollars & cents. Subtracts dollars & cents. Solves word problems	Multiplies dollars & cents. Divides dollars & cents. Identifies relationship between money & decimals. Solves word problems			
TIME	Reads numerals to 12 on clock face	Tells time to the hour. Identifies: days, weeks, months	Tells time to the 1/2 hour. Solves word problems	Tells time in 15 minute intervals, 5 minute intervals. Solves word problems	Tells time in minute intervals: A.M. P.M. Solves word problems	Adds time units. Subtracts time units. Solves word problems	Identifies: decade, score, century, time zones			
SYSTEMS of MEASUREMENT		Uses arbitrary units of length. Reads thermometer	Identifies: centimeter, decimeter, meter, inch, foot, yard, cup, pint, quart. Solves word problems	Identifies: half gallon, gallon	Identifies: ounce, pound. Converts to larger or smaller units. Solves word problems	Adds mile. Measures to nearest specified unit. Constructs scale drawings. Uses F and C thermometers	Estimates measure	Identifies: grams, kilograms. Adds measurements of length. Finds: perimeter, area, volume problems	Multiplies & divides measurement. Finds circumference of circles	Uses decimals in measurement. Solves word problems
GEOMETRY	Identifies plane figures square, rectangle, triangle, circle, ellipse	Identifies solid shapes: cone, cylinder, cube, sphere, pyramid, ellipsoid, rectangular prism. Identifies plane & bilateral symmetry	Identifies: angle, vertex, ray	Identifies: open & closed curves, straight lines, line segments, points	Identifies plane figures for solids	Constructs solid figures	Identifies polygons. Solves word problems	Identifies: edges, faces of geometric shapes, terms used with a circle. Uses a compass	Uses a protractor. Compares angles. Finds sums of angles	Draws parallel & perpendicular lines. Distinguishes between congruent triangles & similar triangles
SPECIAL TOPICS			Identifies: Roman numerals to XII. Constructs bar graphs	Identifies: Roman numerals to XX. Uses bar graphs. Identifies vocabulary for bar graphs	Identifies: Roman numerals to L. Graphs data	Identifies: Roman numerals to C. Graphs number pairs	Identifies: Roman numerals to D. Solves word problems using line graphs. Uses base 5	Identifies: Roman numerals to M. Uses negative numbers in graphing. Uses base 3. Adds & subtracts in base 3 & 5	Identifies: dates using Roman numerals. Uses base 2	Uses other bases

continued

graduate level of the university. The Montclair example in their own words states, "The new system is a partial response to the general trend of moving away from the more abstract letter designations for

SCIENCE PROGRESS REPORT — THE MONTCLAIR PUBLIC SCHOOLS, MONTCLAIR, NEW JERSEY

PUPIL · SCHOOL · TEACHER · CONFERENCE DATES

SCIENCE AREAS	LEVEL A	LEVEL B	LEVEL C	LEVEL D	LEVEL E	LEVEL F	LEVEL G	LEVEL H	LEVEL I	LEVEL J
OBSERVING	Identifies colors—red, orange, yellow, green, blue, purple. Names two or more characteristics of objects. Constructs sets based on color, shape, texture & size. Identifies and names temperature ranges using a thermometer. Identifies sets of objects by name or characteristics. Identifies classifications of objects by stating their color names.	Identifies and names the changes that occur when a solid changes to a liquid & vice versa. Distinguishes objects by odor characteristics. Distinguishes between and identifies sweet, sour, salty. Constructs a classification based on similar and different characteristics	Identifies objects using several senses. Records and reads weather conditions using standard symbols & a simple thermometer	Identifies objects which are magnetic. States the color, shape, size of a few kinds of sliding objects. Identifies & names color changes of an object which take place in an hour or less	Describes in tabular & graphic form changes of momentum with colliding objects. Demonstrates how seeds sprout, & records observations on charts or graphs. Identifies various kinds of possible animal locomotion	Identifies root growth & plant parts	Identifies stimuli & animal responses in an environment	Demonstrates that colonies of bacteria can be observed. Identifies controlled conditions & variables from a given statement. Identifies & states what to observe to determine uniform plant growth		Describes differences between objects dropped simultaneously from the same height
SPACE/TIME	Identifies common two-dimensional shapes. Identifies & demonstrates common directions. Identifies body movements other than locomotion	Constructs a diagram of an arrangement of objects. Identifies two-dimensional shapes. Constructs & names two-dimensional shapes. Identifies three-dimensional shapes. Distinguishes & names calendar days & names time on the hour	Identifies line or plane of symmetry. Describes animals in terms of two- and three-dimensional shapes	Identifies & names angles. Compares distances	Distinguishes & names unseen three-dimensional objects from two-dimensional projections. Distinguishes time intervals in minutes & seconds. States & writes time to nearest five minutes	Differentiates differences between lines on flat & curved surfaces	States velocity & distance in some arbitrary units		Constructs two-dimensional representations of spatial figures	Identifies & states changes in position of objects observed relative to position & another observer. States relationship between linear & angular speed
CLASSIFYING	Separates & describes objects classified according to a single characteristic	Constructs a classification based on the use of objects	Constructs a classification of aquarium contents on basis of living & non-living things. Identifies & names variations in objects & organisms having many features in common		Identifies similarities & differences between objects relative to single characteristics. Separates living organisms in an aquarium into sets & subsets	Identifies substances as solids, liquids, or gases	Identifies, states & orders the principal colors & hues		Constructs & identifies classification codes	Constructs & demonstrates classification of objects based on punch card system
MEASURING	Sorts objects into sets of equal lengths & orders objects from longest to shortest		States & demonstrates that various units of measure provide different numerical answers when used to measure a given length. Orders containers by volume using various methods	Identifies & names 3 units of metric measurement: centimeter, decimeter, meter. Orders groups of two-dimensional figures by area. Orders objects of varying weight using equal arm balance with arbitrary units of weight		Estimates & names within 2 units linear dimensions of common objects using metric system. Identifies weight with a spring, weight as a measurable quantity	States & demonstrates relationship between actual size & representative scale. Identifies & names temperature on an arbitrary scale. States temperatures on Celsius & Fahrenheit scales. Demonstrates measurement of liquid volume in metric units	Demonstrates a method for separating components in a mixture according to size. Constructs representations of vectors. States an operational definition for vectors. Demonstrates that liquid volume can be determined by using the drop as a unit of measure		Identifies & states rate of change using measured units
USING NUMBERS	Identifies equivalent & non-equivalent sets by pairing	Identifies, names & orders members of a set up to 12	Identifies & names positive & negative integers 0 to 9, -9, & 0-99. Constructs new sets of objects by combining 2 sets; states their positions on the numberline	Identifies & names numbers in sequence 0-99. Constructs new sets of objects by combining 2 sets & writes number in new set not exceeding 99	Demonstrates how to determine the sum of any 2 integers from -9 to +9 using numberline	Demonstrates process of finding product of any two numbers 0 to 9 by using repeated addition	States & demonstrates how to find averages	Identifies fractional parts & writes numeral represented. Identifies, orders & names fractions		States meters, decimeters, centimeters in all 3 units. Counts money in decimal notation. Identifies & constructs representations of natural numbers in terms of scientific notation
COMMUNICATING	Uses numerals to describe ordered arrangements. Identifies & names the order position in a sequence of 5 objects or events		Distinguishes identifying characteristics of an object	Constructs & reads bar graphs	Identifies & names changes in characteristics of inflated objects. Identifies observable changes in plants in response to stimuli. Describes growth & changes in living & non-living things	Constructs a bar graph from a frequency distribution	Demonstrates & states in appropriate units the rotational speed of revolving disk. Identifies & names changes in length & direction of shadows		Constructs & interprets coordinate maps. Identifies position of an ordered number pair or graph or grid. Describes an observed experiment in a prescribed manner	Constructs coordinate graph of experimental data of paired events or variables
PREDICTING						Makes predictions based on graphed data. Demonstrates how to test these predictions		Demonstrates methods of collecting & organizing data & predicting from it. Predicts & applies a rule relating to drop heights of various objects	Constructs a graph for prediction, using distance & area in a field of vision as variables. Constructs predictions based on observations contained in a repetitive pattern	
INFERRING						Distinguishes between statements of observation & inference. States reasons for making inferences			Distinguishes between an observation & an inference. Demonstrates that inferences may be altered by additional observations. States observations which can be used to test inferences	Identifies inferences based on observations that inferences can result from sets of experiments

pupil achievement. It represents a movement towards something much more specific for the purpose of tracing a student's academic progress. Each profile provides a carefully developed sequence of skills set up in chart form for each of the three major subject areas."

INDEPENDENT SCHOOL DISTRICT 279
OSSEO, MINNESOTA

NAME ....

SCHOOL ....

TEACHER ....

GRADE FOUR FIVE or SIX
(Circle)

PRINCIPAL ....

Message to Parents: This check list is marked on your child's own ability. It does not indicate his standing in the group. His progress is indicated by a check (x) in the appropriate column. Areas not covered during this working period have been left blank.

	FALL		MIDYEAR		FINAL	
	PROGRESS ACCEPTABLE FOR THIS PUPIL	AREAS WHICH NEED TO BE STRENGTHENED	PROGRESS ACCEPTABLE FOR THIS PUPIL	AREAS WHICH NEED TO BE STRENGTHENED	PROGRESS ACCEPTABLE FOR THIS PUPIL	AREAS WHICH NEED TO BE STRENGTHENED

LANGUAGE ARTS

Reading   Book Level   Fall   Midyear   Final

READING
- Oral reading
- Word recognition
- Vocabulary development
- Practices dictionary skills
- Shows interest in library reading
- Comprehension

Comments:

LANGUAGE
- Oral expression
- Language skills
- Shows creative ability and imagination

Comments:

SPELLING
- Shows mastery of basic spelling list
- Spells accurately in his daily writing

Comments:

HANDWRITING
- Written work is legible
- Written work is neat

Comments:

MATHEMATICS
Knows necessary basic facts of:
- addition and subtraction
- multiplication and division
- fractions, decimals
- Shows mastery of basic processes
- Has success with word problems
- Shows accuracy in computation

Comments:

SOCIAL STUDIES
- Shows an understanding of basic concepts
- Interest in current affairs and problems
- Maps, globes and charts interpretation

Comments:

continued

Authors' Note: The Osseo pupil progress report is another example of a school system moving away from the traditional letter or number grade and using a skill achievement criteria.

	FALL		MIDYEAR		FINAL	
	PROGRESS ACCEPTABLE FOR THIS PUPIL	AREAS WHICH NEED TO BE STRENGTHENED	PROGRESS ACCEPTABLE FOR THIS PUPIL	AREAS WHICH NEED TO BE STRENGTHENED	PROGRESS ACCEPTABLE FOR THIS PUPIL	AREAS WHICH NEED TO BE STRENGTHENED

SCIENCE AND HEALTH
Understands basic science/health concepts
Shows an active interest
Personal health habits

Comments:

MUSIC
Participates to the best of his ability
Understands fundamentals
Listens and appreciates

Comments:

ART
Shows originality
Uses materials well
Enjoys and appreciates

Comments:

PHYSICAL EDUCATION
Displays good sportsmanship
Participates to the best of his abilities

Comments:

WORK HABITS
Works well with others
Works independently
Listens to and follows directions
Takes part in class discussions and activities
Makes good use of time
Is neat
Finishes work on time
Uses research skills

Comments:

SOCIAL ATTITUDES
Respects rights and property of others
Respects authority (obeys rules)
Is courteous and considerate
Practices self-discipline
Shows a good attitude toward school

Comments:

Parents' Signature   Fall ....   Grade Next Year......................

                      Midyear ....

MARKING GUIDE:
√ Where checked, progress is being made
X Where "X" refer to comment

SCIENCE

	1	2	3	4
1. Participates as a group member				
2. Works independently				
3. Identifies main ideas				
4. Uses scientific procedures				
5. Completes assignments				

HEALTH AND SAFETY

	1	2	3	4
1. Follows safety regulations				
2. Knows own physical traits				
3. Takes care of personal hygiene				

PHYSICAL EDUCATION

	1	2	3	4
1. Demonstrates growth in motor skills				
2. Participates in group activities				

ART

	1	2	3	4
1. Demonstrates growth in use of art materials				
2. Participates in art activities				

MUSIC

	1	2	3	4
1. Demonstrates growth in music skills				
2. Participates in music activities				

Caldwell, New Jersey

MARKING GUIDE:
√ Where checked, progress is being made
X Where "X" refer to comment

LANGUAGE ARTS

	1	2	3	4
1. Utilizes word attack skills				
2. Shows vocabulary growth				
3. Comprehends written materials				
4. Reads critically				
5. Utilizes library facilities				
6. Utilizes dictionary skills				
7. Expresses ideas clearly, orally				
8. Expresses written ideas clearly				
9. Utilizes listening skills				
10. Writes legibly				
11. Spells words correctly				
12. Completes assignments				

SOCIAL STUDIES

	1	2	3	4
1. Participates as a group member				
2. Works independently				
3. Identifies main ideas				
4. Uses a variety of resources				
5. Completes assignments				

MARKING GUIDE:
√ Where checked, progress is being made
X Where "X" refer to comment

SOCIAL BEHAVIOR

	1	2	3	4
1. Practices self-control; self discipline				
2. Cooperates in work and play				
3. Adapts to changing roles in group situations				
4. Accepts responsibility				
5. Respects personal/public property				

STUDY SKILLS

	1	2	3	4
1. Makes plans to guide his learning				
2. Follows directions—written and oral				
3. Works independently				
4. Enters discussions				
5. Uses time, materials wisely				

MATHEMATICS

	1	2	3	4
1. Knows basic facts				
2. Uses basic operations				
3. Solves mathematical problems				
4. Shows accuracy in computations				
5. Applies knowledge to practical situations				
6. Completes assignments				

Caldwell-West Caldwell Schools

Authors' Note: The Caldwell example is similar to the Osseo report with some variations in the skills covered. This minor variation is fruitful as an expression of faculty study and not simply as a "copy" of another school district's reporting system.

writing skills

SKILL	GRADES K-2	GRADES 3-4	GRADES 5-6	GRADES 7-8
Writing vocabulary	Makes personal dictionary; asks about words he doesn't know; recognizes some synonyms; uses comparison words	Injects color words and phrases into sentences; recognizes more synonyms and some antonyms; shows interest in word choices; begins to use dictionary	Uses more precise terms; avoids trite expressions; keeps list of new words; is accurate in descriptions; uses color and mood words	Includes simple figures of speech in writing; writes free from cliches and jargon; uses multiforms of words; relies on dictionary; changes words to make copy more interesting or accurate
Sentence structure	Contributes ideas to experience chart; begins sentences with capital letters and closes them with correct marks; subjects and verbs agree in sentences	Makes sentence fragments into sentences; can correct incorrect sentences; shows growth in use of modifiers; begins to use compound and complex sentences; composes story without change in tense	Proofreads for sentence structure; recognizes subordinate ideas; shows variety in sentence structure; joins subordinating ideas	Uses correct tense and subject and number agreement; uses adverbial and adjective forms correctly; subordinates phrases to both nouns and verbs; uses correct plural form of nouns
Construction of a paragraph	Tells or writes several related sentences on a topic	Adds to a topic sentence; picks out nonrelated sentences from a paragraph; can write a "how to" paragraph	Makes a simple outline and writes from it; proofreads paragraph and rewrites it; writes two- or three-paragraph account of an event	Listens to material and recognizes where paragraphs occur; paragraphs dialogue correctly; shows growth in relating ideas to each other; can bring a paragraph to a climax

Carole Whiston • Margaret Morton
Helen E. Bailey
Teachers and Librarian, Longfellow School

assisted by

Elinor Yungmeyer
Consultant, Library Services

Oak Park Schools, Oak Park, Illinois

REPRINTED WITH PERMISSION OF INSTRUCTOR
THE INSTRUCTOR PUBLICATIONS, INC., DANSVILLE, NEW YORK

continued

Authors' Note: Content and behavioral goals for writing skills in a form that is easily understood by parents, teachers and students. It will assist the teacher in parent-teacher conferences

Organization of thoughts and ideas	Rearranges short jumbled sentences; puts events in correct order; plays games requiring "Yes, I did" or "No, I didn't" answers	Can hear ideas and then propose topic sentence; lists points under a main topic; suggests title	Organizes a report for social studies or science; uses notes from several sources in a report; edits out irrelevant ideas	Makes plot for play; makes outline for book report or story; organizes a committee report; writes headline for outlines
Standards for writing	Copies simple story neatly; uses picture dictionary to confirm spelling; keeps paper clean	Places heading on paper; has margins; can position headings and shows indentations; recognizes spelling difficulties; handwriting is legible	Reorganizes and rewrites untidy paper; shows growth in handwriting; proofreads for punctuation and capitals; uses dictionary for unknown words	Writes legibly with reasonable speed; checks papers for neatness and arrangement; keeps list of spelling difficulty; avoids excessive erasures; organizes loose-leaf notebook
Abilities to observe	Identifies objects in room; draws members of family, home, and other familiar scenes; includes details when describing event	Tells story based on picture; copies a letter accurately; plays simple games based on recall	Observes and describes nature forms; hears commonplace noises and writes about them; notices and identifies color differences	Can keep an observation diary; detects small differences in size, shape, placement, and colors; can write a description or answer questions after seeing a picture
Prose and poetry	Contributes ideas for a story; names words or phrases that express mood or emotion	Composes two-line rhymes; begins to write dialogue and stories; can end an unfinished story; keeps writing in notebook or class scrapbook	Constructs limericks and four-line verses; "thinks up" plot ideas; writes a narrative of several paragraphs; can write simple play; uses both direct and indirect discourse	Attempts longer verse (with or without rhyme); can compose beginning to a finished story; writes for school paper; keeps personal journal of original writing; writes play with several scenes; writes a newspaper account
Practical writing	Recognizes writing as a form; writes name, address, and telephone number; composes simple invitations, thank-you messages	Can develop a simple chart; writes a written request, notice, or announcement; hears verbal instructions and then writes them; prepares simple book report	Constructs and lists a set of directions; keeps class or committee minutes; takes notes as he reads and prepares report from them; takes notes on field trip and writes up an account; writes business letters	Composes paragraph answers to thought questions; prepares interesting "how to" articles; writes variety of business letters

**Carole Whiston • Margaret Morton
Helen E. Bailey**
Teachers and Librarian, Longfellow School

assisted by
Elinor Yungmeyer
Consultant, Library Services
Oak Park Schools, Oak Park, Illinois

REPRINTED WITH PERMISSION OF INSTRUCTOR
THE INSTRUCTOR PUBLICATIONS, INC., DANSVILLE, NEW YORK

by providing exact and clearly understandable goals for discussion. It will assist the teacher in avoiding negative terminology by providing positive directions in showing pupil progress.

Behavioral Goals
of
General Education
in
High School *

1.442 Recognizes need for taking personal interest in, and responsibility for, conservation of natural resources.

Illustrative Behaviors

(a) Studies current problems of production, consumption, and distribution of natural resources as a way of becoming more intelligently participative in the work-life of the world.

(b) Obeys laws and rules made to conserve natural resources, fire-prevention, reforestation, preservation of wildlife, land, conservation, etc. *

(c) Is careful and economical in his use of materials—clothing, food, school and home equipment, books and school supplies. *

(d) Forms tentative judgments as to how society can fulfill its responsibility for conserving human and material resources.

(e) Understands the issues involved in the wise and intelligent development of natural resources. *

RUSSELL SAGE FOUNDATION
New York

*By WILL FRENCH
and Associates

Authors' Note: Conservation is a most "timely-relevant" topic for all schools. The national climate —i.e. the President's comments, congressional committees, national television and radio programs, newspapers and magazines—has made this topic one of great concern to administrators and teachers, but particularly to students. The behavioral goals listed here will serve as a beginning for the faculty's discussions.

National Assessment of Educational Progress
Citizenship Objectives

VII. SUPPORT RATIONALITY IN COMMUNICATION, THOUGHT AND ACTION ON SOCIAL PROBLEMS.

The habit of approaching problems rationally should have begun to form by age 9. This approach includes being informed and open-minded, communicating with others, and thinking independently. In 13-year-olds rational thought is rapidly developing toward its full capacity. Although their own personal lives are still their main concern, they should be gaining information, communicating, and thinking independently about broader matters of social interest. Seventeen-year-olds or adults realize that if informed rationality is the most promising approach to problem-solving, then in a democracy, it is essential that informed rationality be widespread among the citizenry, for in the long run the burden of solving society's problems is theirs. Universal education and free, open communication help a society to solve its problems rationally, first, by stimulating the spread of wisdom as widely and quickly as possible, and consequently by the more enlightened judgments which the citizenry conveys to its leaders and policy-makers.

A. *Try to inform themselves on socially important matters and to understand alternative viewpoints.*

Age 9 They ask questions and, if needed, probe for more complete answers by further questioning; they do this with other students, teachers, counselors, parents, and especially with persons who have unique experience or expertise to share. They have the habit of listening attentively and open-mindedly to what any other person may say without pre-judging its merit. They recognize that there are many sides to a story or question. They show an expanding awareness of the world outside their own immediate group or environment; they recognize the major problems facing most of the world, e.g., war, poverty, disease, food and water. They make use of available sources of information such as books, magazines, newspapers, TV, radio, teachers, parents, and authorities, and are aware that a single source may present only one side of a story.

Age 13 (in addition to Age 9)

They seek full understanding of the several sides of an issue, and are aware of some of the facts and opposing arguments in such current controversies as racial integration, teenage idols, and the quality of television programs.

Age 17 They ask questions and, if needed, probe for more complete answers by discussion and further questions; they do this with other students, teachers, counselors, parents, and especially with persons who have unique experience or expertise to share. They have the habit of listening attentively and open-mindedly to what any other person may say without pre-judging its merit. They seek full understanding of the several sides of an issue, and are aware of the more relevant facts and cogent opposing arguments in such current controversies as racial integration, U.S. foreign policy, problems of the economy, sexual mores, and individualism vs. social organization. They make use of available sources of information such as books, magazines, newspapers, TV, radio, teachers, and authorities, trying not to rely on a single source in important matters.

Adult They ask questions and, if needed, probe for more complete answers by discussion and further questions; they do this with friends, work associates, civic leaders, and especially with persons who have unique experience or expertise to share. They have the habit of listening attentively and open-mindedly to what any other person may say without pre-judging its merit, even if they have previously committed themselves to a contrary cause or plan of action. They seek full understanding of the several sides of an issue, and are aware of relevant facts and cogent opposing arguments in such current controversies as racial integration, U.S. foreign policy, problems of the economy, sexual mores, and individualism vs. social organization. They make use of available sources of information such as books, magazines, newspapers, TV, radio, and authorities, trying not to rely on a single source in important matters.

B. *Evaluate communications critically and form their own opinions independently.*

Age 9 They question the authority or evidence for doubtful assertions, such as rumors or advertising claims. They recognize grossly illogical statements. They are not easily influenced or swayed by other students' evaluative judgments, but do not hesitate to change their opinion when their own error dawns on them. They do not accept or reject views simply because an emotional label (e.g., "Communist") has been ascribed. They are beginning to form their own values and beliefs.

Age 13 They question the authority or evidence for doubtful assertions, such as rumors or advertising claims. They recognize and challenge illogical arguments. They are not easily influenced or swayed by others' evaluative judgments, but do not hesitate to change their opinions in the light of convincing new information. They are forming their own values and beliefs in relation to those of family and friends. They do not accept or reject views simply because an emotional label (e.g., "Communist") has been ascribed.

Age 17 When faced with contradictory information or a rumor they seek verification rather than passing it on unquestioned as truth. They question the authority or evidence for doubtful assertions, especially political accusations and advertising claims, and evaluate the adequacy of such authority or evidence realistically. They recognize and challenge illogical arguments. They are not easily influenced or swayed by others' evaluative judgments, but do not hesitate to change their opinions in the light of convincing new evidence. They form their own values and beliefs by integrating their own unique experience with all relevant information. They do not accept or reject views simply because an emotional label (e.g., "Communist") has been ascribed.

Adult (as for Age 17)

Committee on Assessing the Progress of Education
Room 201A Huron Towers
2222 Fuller Road
Ann Arbor, Michigan

continued

Authors' Note: The formation of goal statements that reflect different age groups is most difficult to find. The National Committee on Assessment has done a most worthwhile task in formulating such behavioral goals. The two illustrations are magnificently phrased and deal with topics of great concern to elementary teachers: (1) the need for "approaching problems rationally" and "independent thinking"; (2) "taking responsibility for one's own personal development and obligations."

National Assessment of Educational Progress
Citizenship Objectives

C. *Weigh alternatives and consequences carefully, then make decisions and carry them out without undue delay.*

Age 9   They understand the importance of collecting accurate information and withhold a decision if awaiting further information is likely to be worth the delay. They devote time and effort to important decisions, while more routine decisions are reached without undue worry or procrastination. They can carry out a complex task with efficiency, using all available resources; e.g., making a classroom chart which displays samples of leaves of all locally native trees.

Age 13   They understand the importance to decision-making of collecting accurate information and withhold a decision if awaiting further information is likely to be worth the delay. Daily decisions such as how to spend leisure time or when to do homework are reached without undue worry or procrastination. They can carry out a task or organize a group project with efficiency, using all available resources. Given a complex task, such as planning routes and exits for a fire drill, or assigning and scheduling clean-up duties where the duties are interrelated, they can outline a sensible plan for carrying it out.

Age 17   In making civic and social decisions they examine alternatives and weigh consequences in terms of all their relevant values and loyalties. They understand the importance to decision-making of collecting accurate information, and withhold a decision if awaiting further information is likely to be worth the delay. However, the time and effort they give to a decision is roughly proportional to the *importance* of the decision. More routine decisions such as how to spend leisure time or when to do homework are reached without undue worry or procrastination. They can carry out a task or organize a group project with efficiency, using all available resources. Given a complex task, such as getting the whole student body to a distant location and back, or getting community agreement on the choice of school colors, they can outline a sensible plan for carrying it out.

Adult   In making civic and social decisions they examine alternatives and weigh the consequences in terms of all their relevant values and loyalties. They recognize that a single decision often involves conflicting values or loyalties (e.g., job vs. family, nation vs. religion, freedom vs. security) and face them rationally, neither rejecting one value outright nor trying to ignore it. They are not drawn into hasty action by the emotional fervor of an excited group or mob. They understand the importance to decision-making of collecting accurate information, and withhold a decision if awaiting further information is likely to be worth the delay. However, the time and effort they give to a decision is roughly proportional to the *importance* of the decision. They can carry out a task or organize a group project with efficiency, using all available resources. Given a complex task, such as coordinating a charity fund drive, or informing the community of a planned event, they can outline a sensible plan for carrying it out.

D. *See relations among social problems and have good ideas for solutions.*

Age 9   None

Age 13   Given a school or social problem, they can draw on related problems and name many factors that should be considered in deciding on a solution. Their ideas for solving such problems are sensible and they do not accept pat answers for complex social problems such as poverty, war, and racial conflict.

Age 17   They see parallels between national and international problems and their own interpersonal relations (e.g., conflict, law and order, rights and freedoms). They can see important differences between two social phenomena such as picketing and rioting; they can also recognize underlying similarities, contributing causes, and possible effects. Given social problems, they can draw on related problems and name many factors that should be considered in deciding on a solution. Their ideas for solving such problems are ingenious and/or workable, and they do not accept pat answers for complex social problems such as poverty, war, racial conflict, and corruption.

Adult   (as for Age 17)

E. *Support free communication and communicate honestly with others.*

Age 9   They willingly and clearly express their own views on school and social matters, and encourage open discussion of all issues. They give honest rather than socially desirable answers, even if it means disagreeing with the group. They do not distort facts nor misrepresent others' viewpoints.

Age 13   (as for Age 9)

Age 17   They recognize the following values of communication: becoming aware of others' viewpoints, increasing one's own store of knowledge, keeping an open mind, testing one's own opinions and theories, making better civic decisions, gaining practice in expressing thoughts to others, and causing others to evaluate their own ideas. They believe in full disclosure of all information of civic concern; they protest when unethical behavior is concealed to protect the guilty from embarrassment. They encourage the hearing of dissenting viewpoints among friends, in school, at work, and at public meetings. They disapprove of censorship aimed at the general public and the suppression of certain views, books, and movies on the pretext that they might mislead, brainwash, anger or arouse "other people," whether suppression is by school or public officials, by the press and media, or by self-appointed censorship committees. They see the dangers of having all newspapers and mass media controlled by the same few persons. They willingly and clearly express their own views on civic and social matters, however controversial the issue. They encourage and participate in open discussions; they give honest rather than socially desirable answers, even if it means disagreeing with the group. They do not distort facts nor misrepresent others' viewpoints. They do not stop communicating altogether with someone just because they disagree. They help circulate widely facts and beliefs that might have civic impact by writing letters to editors or representatives, telephoning others in the community, helping to publish or circulate printed matter, and by frank discussions. They advocate new sources and types of public information where needed.

Committee on Assessing the Progress of Education
Room 201A Huron Towers
2222 Fuller Road
Ann Arbor, Michigan

continued

National Assessment of Educational Progress
Citizenship Objectives

Adult (in addition to Age 17)

They favor open press and media coverage of governmental operations.

F. *Understand the role of education in developing good citizens.*

Age 9 They appreciate educational achievements of their own and of other students. They understand how education and free communication can help people make wiser decisions about their government, and that education can help each person make the best use of his ability.

Age 13 (as for Age 9)

Age 17 They believe that more intelligent civic decisions can be made by a citizenry which has acquired a broader perspective on social problems through formal education. They are aware of instances of poorly educated populations being exploited by their governments. They understand the following arguments for universal education: The economic vitality of the nation depends on maximum utilization of everyone's ability; rational participation by citizens strengthens a democratic government; children whose parents are least able and willing to provide them a formal education are often those who need it most.

Adult (in addition to Age 17)

They encourage and praise educational achievement by their families and friends.

VIII. TAKE RESPONSIBILITY FOR OWN PERSONAL DEVELOPMENT AND OBLIGATIONS.

Even 9-year-olds have personal obligations to others; fulfilling these reliably is important not only for its immediate civic value but also as a way of developing worthy habits and character traits for later life. They may also increase their social usefulness by taking advantage of school and other learning opportunities. In addition, 13-year-olds should take full advantage of their educational opportunities in awareness that what they learn will be of value in adult civic and occupational roles. Seventeen-year-olds should recognize they will soon be adults, and bear the full legal, moral, and social responsibility for their actions. To prepare themselves for adult roles and responsibilities they should take advantage of school and the guidance of their parents. For adults, this objective concerns the part of their private lives and careers that has direct implications for the welfare of others.

A. Ages 9, 13, 17: *Further their own self-improvement and education.*

Adult: *Continue their own education and self-improvement and are occupationally useful to society.*

Age 9 They take the initiative to learn as much as they can, in school and elsewhere. They use school and community libraries. They complete homework assignments on time, and follow instructions in class. When absent, they make up work missed. They seek help from teachers, parents, or other students, when having difficulty in understanding work. They develop creative hobbies. They take advantage of other sources of education outside school—e.g., books, magazines, films, radio and TV, museums, observatories, and travel.

Age 13 They explore different fields to better learn their own interests and talents. They seek to learn as much as they can rather than to get by with the least effort. They schedule time spend on studies and on different types of recreation, and often combine companionship with other activities. They take advantage of school and community libraries. They complete homework assignments and follow instructions in class. When absent, they take initiative to make up work missed. They seek help from teachers, parents, or other students when having difficulty understanding school work. They take part in extracurricular activities and creative hobbies. They take advantage of other sources of education outside school—e.g., books, magazines, films, radio and TV, museums, observatories, and travel.

Age 17 They exploit and develop their talents to the maximum, and they seek to learn as much as they can rather than to get by with the least effort. They explore different fields to better learn their own interests and talents. They schedule time spent on studies and on different types of recreation, and often combine companionship with other activities. They take advantage of school and community libraries. They complete homework assignments and follow instructions in class. When absent, they take initiative to make up work missed. They arrange conferences with teachers when having difficulty in understanding work, and talk to teachers during free time, either on class-related subjects or topics of general interst. They take part in extracurricular activities, and creative hobbies. They take advantage of other sources of education outside school—e.g., books, periodicals, correspondence courses, films, lectures, radio and TV, concerts, museums and observatories, and travel.

Adult They evaluate their own abilities and achievements realistically; and they exploit their talents to the maximum. They take advantage of the community library and other adult education facilities, and support community programs for adult education. They try to develop additional skills in case their present job or occupation becomes obsolete. Personal rewards and opportunity being about equal, they choose to engage in an occupation or business which better serves community and national needs. They take advantage of freedom of enterprise by inventing, producing, or marketing useful products and services.

B. *Plan ahead for major life changes.*

Age 9 None

Age 13 None

Age 17 Before making serious decisions about marriage, religion, military service, commitment to a new responsibility, future education or occupation, they seek relevant information and counsel, and consider alternatives and consequences carefully. They try to find out what kinds of job opportunities the future holds, what such jobs are like, what education is needed for them; they consult about opportunities with school counselors and parents. They try to evaluate their own abilities and achievements realistically in terms of adult roles. They discuss, with parents and adult friends, financial problems and responsibilities of adult life: taxes; cost of food, clothing, housing, insurance; occupational salary ranges. They take school courses appropriate to intended adult roles, and

Committee on Assessing the Progress of Education
Room 201A Huron Towers
2222 Fuller Road
Ann Arbor, Michigan

continued

National Assessment of Educational Progress
Citizenship Objectives

participate in work, training, or other experiences which could reasonably contribute to success in adult occupation (e.g., cooking and housekeeping at home).

Adult They are willing to forego some immediate pleasures for long-term goals. They plan for the future financial needs of their dependents and save or invest wisely to meet those needs. They start preparing well in advance for such contingencies as death, illness, disability, and retirement. They are willing to accept change in their civic and personal environments, and are prepared to cope with it.

C. *Are conscientious, dependable, self-disciplined, and value excellence and initiative.*

Age 9 They are not careless or tardy in keeping appointments. They keep promises, and can be trusted with minor responsibilities. They correct their own errors, and do not blame others for their mistakes. They persevere until a job is completed. They plan the use of money to allow for past commitments and probable future needs as well as present desires.

Age 13 (in addition to Age 9)

They take initiative to earn some money in ways approved by parents. They understand that with more freedom goes more responsibility, and can be trusted with moderate responsibilities.

Age 17 They adhere to their own moral and ethical codes rather than giving them lip service only. They repay debts and live up to pledges to church, charities or other organizations. They take advantage of our free enterprise system by inventing, producing, or marketing useful products and services. They seek part-time or summer jobs (e.g., baby-sitter, gardener, tutor, lifeguard, musician with dance band, sales clerk, construction worker, usher, office worker or secretary, gas station attendant). At work they follow agreed upon procedures and schedules, and persevere until a job is completed. They are willing to work extra hours on occasion and to undertake additional responsibilities. They start new tasks without having to be told, check work for mistakes, and use initiative to find better ways of achieving work goals. They are not careless or tardy in keeping appointments. They correct their own errors, and do not blame others for their mistakes. They budget use of time and money to allow for commitments, expenses, and probable future needs. They understand that with more freedom goes more reponsibility.

Adult They adhere to their moral and ethical codes rather than giving them lip service only. They repay debts, pay bills and taxes promptly, and live up to pledges to church, charities or other organizations. At work they follow agreed upon procedures and schedules. They take pride in the quality of their workmanship, services or products. They are willing to work extra hours on occasion and to undertake additional responsibilities. They start new tasks without having to be told, check work for mistakes, and use initiative to find better ways of achieving work goals. They are not careless or wasteful, nor tardy in keeping appointments. They correct their own errors, and do not blame others for their mistakes.

D. *Economically support self and dependents.*

Age 9 None

Age 13 None

Age 17 None

Adult As head of household, they provide financial support for their families to the best of their abilities. They continually seek gainful employment if possible, rather than depending indefinitely on unemployment compensation or welfare payments. They consider the reasonable current financial needs of other members of the family along with necessary expenses and plan their budgets accordingly. They shop economically.

Committee on Assessing the Progress of Education
Room 201A Huron Towers
2222 Fuller Road
Ann Arbor, Michigan

INSTRUCTIONAL OBJECTIVES
EXCHANGE CATALOG

Sample Objectives

READING

Major Category:	Word Recognition- Phonetic Analysis Grade Introduced: K
Sub-Category:	Rhyming Words 10X Acceptability Rating: 2

OBJECTIVE: After listening to a group of words, some of which rhyme and some of which do not, the student will orally designate the rhyming and non-rhyming words.

SAMPLE ITEM: Listen to each of the following lists. After each one, state which words do not rhyme.

1. make, big, fake, take
2. fill, bill, kite, mill
3. sat, cat, tell, mat

ANSWERS:
1. big
2. kite
3. tell

ENGLISH LITERATURE

Major Category:	Poetry Grade Introduced: Senior High
Sub-Category:	Tone 10X Acceptability Rating:

Toward is defined as the attitude of the poet toward his subject matter or toward his audience. The tone of a poem may be formal, informal, solemn, ironic, horror-stricken, sarcastic, humorous, or playful.

OBJECTIVE: The student will demonstrate an understanding of what is meant by tone in poetry and how tone is achieved in a poem. That is, when given a poem, the student will be able to describe the attitude contained therein toward the subject matter or the audience and identify the means by which the tone is revealed.

SAMPLE ITEM: In "Apparently With No Surprise" by Emily Dickenson, what is the speaker's attitude toward nature? What details reveal the tone?

CRITERIA: The speaker's attitude is one of dismay. The speaker presents a picture of a world apparently governed by whim, without purpose or compassion. The frost kills the flower "in accidental power" and the rest of nature appears undisturbed. The sun "proceeds unmoved" and the flower itself does not seem surprised. Even God seems to be "approving."

MATHEMATICS

Major Category:	Applications, Problem Solving Grade Introduced: 7
Sub-Category:	Statistics 10X Acceptability Rating: 2

OBJECTIVE: Given a situation in which a faulty conclusion is presented, the student will analyze the data and identify the errors in logic.

SAMPLE ITEM: What is wrong with the conclusion based on the given data? More people were killed in airplane accidents in 1969 than in 1929.

ANSWER: There were less planes in 1929. It is better to talk about the percentage of deaths in relation to the number of air miles flown in these two years.

University of California
Center for the Study of Evaluation
Instructional Objectives Exchange
145 Moore Hall
Los Angeles, California 90024

Authors' Note: Instructional objectives for each of the subject areas is one of the hoped-for results of the elementary school evaluation. The development of criteria for this purpose is most difficult for the average school faculty. However, it is one of the fruitful tasks of a study group for it forces the faculty to look at the "end product" in general behavioral terms rather than in specific achievement items.

II. NATURE OF OFFERINGS

Checklist

The music courses:

1. Extend the knowledge, skills, and attitudes developed in previous years. na 1 2 3 4
2. Involve activities appropriate to the individual needs and abilities of students. na 1 2 3 4
3. Provide an opportunity for recognition and encouragement of individual achievement. na 1 2 3 4
4. Bring worthwhile programs in the community to the attention of students. na 1 2 3 4
5. Continue opportunities to develop skill and ability in reading music. na 1 2 3 4
6. Provide for development of basic music skills for students who may have had no previous training. na 1 2 3 4
7. Provide, in unison and part singing, for the particular needs of the changing voice. na 1 2 3 4
8. Provide for groups such as duets, quartets, octets, and other small ensembles. na 1 2 3 4
9. Provide exploratory experience with a variety of musical instruments. na 1 2 3 4
10. Provide opportunities to listen to recordings of many types of music. na 1 2 3 4
11. Provide opportunities to listen to other students perform. na 1 2 3 4
12. Provide opportunities to study a wide range of music of various periods, styles, nationalities, forms, composers, and media. na 1 2 3 4

13. Provide an opportunity for students to understand the historical and cultural milieu in which the music being studied was created. na 1 2 3 4
14. Emphasize understanding of music as an expression of religious faith. na 1 2 3 4
15. Provide an opportunity for talented students to learn to improvise, compose, arrange, and conduct. na 1 2 3 4
16. Provide opportunity to cooperate with other departments in presentation of school performances and programs. na 1 2 3 4
17. Provide for the development of student leadership in music. na 1 2 3 4
18. Provide a balanced music program in which no phase is unduly emphasized. na 1 2 3 4
19. Provide opportunity for students with broad musical interests to study both instrumental and vocal music. na 1 2 3 4
20. Provide opportunities for class instruction in stringed, wind, percussion, and keyboard instruments, and voice. na 1 2 3 4
21. Include classes in music history and theory. na 1 2 3 4
22. na 1 2 3 4

Supplementary Data

1. Describe any innovative or unusual phases of course content or teaching methodology.

2. Describe any limitations in the music offerings.

Evaluations

a) *How well does the variety of music offerings meet the needs of all students?* na 1 2 3 4
b) *How well does the quality of music offerings meet the needs of all students?* na 1 2 3 4
c) *How adequate is the offering in vocal music?* na 1 2 3 4
d) *How adequate is the offering in stringed instrument music?* na 1 2 3 4
e) *How adequate is the offering in wind and percusssion instrument music?* na 1 2 3 4
f) *How well are music courses correlated with other courses?* na 1 2 3 4
g) *How well are music courses adapted to individual aptitudes and abilities of participating students?* na 1 2 3 4
h) *To what extent are opportunities provided for talented students to realize their optimum potential in musical performance, understanding, and creativity?* na 1 2 3 4

EVALUATIVE CRITERIA
Fourth Edition

by National Study of Secondary School Evaluation, *1785 Massachusetts Avenue, N.W., Washington, D.C. 20036. All rights reserved. No part of this material may be reproduced in any form without prior written permission of the publisher.*

Author's Note: The evaluating of a specific offering has many aspects: such as variety of offerings, adequate correlation with other subjects, adaption to individual needs. This example in the secondary field can be readily adapted for the elementary school.

A GUIDE FOR THE REVIEW OF A PROGRAM IN ELEMENTARY EDUCATION

Educational Communications Media - Materials

	Strong Aspects	Needs Improvement
1. A planned program for the purchase and use of educational communications material is provided.		
2. Teacher committee' participate in the selection of new materials		
3. A person who can be consulted in communications problems, i.e. production of materials, effective use, sources and resources, etc., is available.		
4. Ordering and scheduling of instructional materials are made easy.		
5. Production facilities and materials for preparing self-made instructional materials are available		
6. Instructional materials are of sufficient variety		
7. Instructional materials are sufficiently adequate in quantity, so that their use is effective.		
8. Instructional materials collections are properly cataloged and administered.		
9. Educational communications equipment is of sufficient variety .		
10. Equipment is sufficiently adequate in quantity, so that it is available when needed		
11. Individuals and smaller groups use instruction materials for study and research.		
12. There is a concerted effort to know about newer media (electronic laboratories, 8mm motion pictures, programed instruction, educational television, overhead projectuals, etc.) and to use them when they are appropriate		

Comments on strengths, weaknesses, or plans for improvement:

THE UNIVERSITY OF THE STATE OF NEW YORK
THE STATE EDUCATION DEPARTMENT
COOPERATIVE REVIEW SERVICE
ALBANY, NEW YORK 12224

continued

Authors' Note: The library or multi-media center is usually referred to as the "center" of the school. In reviewing the program it is helpful to have the various components of the program reviewed separately. The New York State Department of Education Guide offers some good hints for the review of the materials of the Media Center as well as the purpose of the library.

A GUIDE FOR THE REVIEW OF A PROGRAM
IN ELEMENTARY EDUCATION

School Library	Strong Aspect	Needs Improvement
1. The school has a central library.		
2. The school has the services of a qualified librarian.		
3. Classroom library collections have appropriate books, pamphlets, and magazines*.		
4. Children are encouraged to take books home.		
5. The book collection for general reading and reference covers all curriculum areas in each grade*		
6. The library serves as a center for other resources, such as films, slides, and pictures		
7. The library is equipped with: Shelving. Tables and chairs Vertical file (legal size). Card catalog. Book trucks Librarian's desk and chair. Bulletin boards Typewriter		
8. The library has a work area or adjacent workroom for processing and repairing books and other curriculum materials		
9. The librarian and teacher work closely together in the selection of reading materials for children's use.		

*The principal should list the amount of the per-pupil appropriation for the current school year.

Comments on strengths, weaknesses, or plans for improvement:

THE UNIVERSITY OF THE STATE OF NEW YORK
THE STATE EDUCATION DEPARTMENT
COOPERATIVE REVIEW SERVICE
ALBANY, NEW YORK 12224

Standards
for
Accrediting
Elementary
Schools
in Virginia

EQUIPMENT AND MATERIALS FOR INSTRUCTION

Library

1. Each library shall contain a balanced collection of at least ten (10) books per child selected from State-approved lists.

2. Each library shall contain a collection of at least fifteen (15) magazines for children and professional personnel and at least one State and one local newspaper.

3. Each school shall have budgeted and expended for library materials an annual appropriation of at least $2.50 per child based on Average Daily Membership.

4. The library shall contain a professional resource area for teachers.

Audio-Visual Equipment

Each school shall have readily available for immediate use in every classroom appropriate audio-visual equipment selected from the following list:

> 16 m.m. projectors
> Filmstrip and Slide projectors
> Overhead projectors
> Opaque projectors
> Microprojectors
> Microscopes
> Record players
> Tape recorders
> Projection screens
> Televisions
> Radios
> Filmstrip viewers
> Carts for projection equipment

Supplementary Materials

1. Appropriate maps and globes shall be readily available for immediate use in every classroom.

2. Each school shall have a collection of recordings, filmstrips, and such other resource materials as pictures, diagrams, charts, and clippings properly organized and maintained as part of the instructional materials center.

3. A variety of multi-level instructional materials shall be available to every classroom.

4. Each school shall have budgeted and expended for instructional materials and supplies, not including basal texts and library materials, an annual appropriation of at least $2.50 per child based on Avearge Daily Membership.

Textbooks

1. Basal textbooks shall be selected from the list approved by the State Board of Education.

2. Teachers shall be provided with a teachers' edition of each basic textbook.

ELEMENTARY EDUCATION SERVICE
STATE DEPARTMENT OF EDUCATION
RICHMOND, VIRGINIA 23216

Authors' Note: State standards for the elementary school library are usually set in terms of minimums. Virginia not only does this but thoughtfully sets out goals for the improvement of the service from the basic acceptable standard.

Standards
for school media
programs

The resources
of the media center:
size and
expenditures

The standards recommended for schools of 250 students or over are as follows:

Books

At least 6000-10,000 titles representing 10,000 volumes or 20 volumes per student, whichever is greater

Magazines

Elementary school (K-6)   40-50 titles (includes some adult non-professional periodicals)

Elementary school (K-8)   50-75 titles
Junior high school   100-125 titles
Secondary school   125-175 titles
All schools   In addition: necessary magazine indexes and duplication of titles and indexes as required

Newspapers

Elementary school   3-6 titles
Junior high school   6-10 titles
Secondary school   6-10 titles
All schools   One local, one state, and one national newspaper to be represented in the collection

Pamphlets, clippings, and miscellaneous materials

Pamphlets, government documents, catalogs of colleges and technical schools, vocational information, clippings, and other materials appropriate to the curriculum and for other interests of students

Filmstrips

500-1000 titles, representing 1500 prints or 3 prints per pupil, whichever is greater (the number of titles to be increased in larger collections)

8mm films
Single concept
Regular length[1]

1½ films per student with at least 500 titles supplemented by duplicates

16mm films

Acquisition of 16mm films at the building level would depend upon extent and frequency of use of individual film titles in the school, upon the availability of a system media center and its collection of film resources, and upon other factors.[2] Whatever the source, the films must be quickly and easily accessible to the students and teachers requiring them. The recommendation given below is stated in terms of accessibility. Recommended: access to a minimum of 3000 titles supplemented by duplicates and rentals

Tape and disc recordings
(excluding electronic laboratory materials)

1000-2000 titles representing 3000 records or tapes or 6 per student, whichever is greater (the number of titles to be increased in larger collections)

1. Because of the nature of certain media forms and the evolving or transitional development of others, quantitative recommendations cannot be given. Nevertheless, these materials make a unique contribution to the instructional program and provide resources for the academic needs and general interests of students. An abundant number should be available in the media center.
2. Absence of a quantitative recommendation should not be interpreted as meaning that it is not desirable for the media center in the individual school to have 16mm films in its collection. Former standards have indicated that a school should purchase films used six or more times a year, and that an annual rental fee for a film totaling from one-fifth to one-seventh of its purchase price generally indicates the feasibility of permanent acquisition. In at least one large metropolitan school system, experience indicated the value of a basic elementary school building collection of 300-400 film titles, with access to a central collection on a daily delivery basis.

continued

Authors' Note: The faculty is always most interested in the standards of the library or multi-media center. It will assist the evaluation if definite standards are used to evaluate the school facilities. The illustration is from the American Library Association and is usually considered to be "the final word" in these matters.

Standards
for school media
programs

The resources
of the media center:
size and
expenditures

Slides	2000 (including all sizes of slides)
Graphic materials	
Art prints (reproductions)	1000 with duplicates as needed
Pictures and study prints	Individual study prints and pictures for the picture and vertical file collections; in addition to individual prints, access to 15 sets per teaching station plus 25 sets available from the media center
Other graphics[1]	Posters, photographs, charts, diagrams, graphs, and other types
Globes	
Elementary school	1 globe in each teaching station and 2 in the media center
Secondary school	1 globe per 5 teaching stations and 2 in the media center
All schools	In addition, special globes to be available in the media center
Maps	1 map for each region studied and special maps (economic, weather, political, historical, and others) for each area studied
	Duplicate maps available for each class section requiring maps at the same time, the number of duplicates to be determined by sections of students and the availability of maps on transparencies and filmstrips
	Wall maps for teaching stations
Microform	To be purchased as available on topics in the curriculum. All periodical subscriptions indexed in *Reader's Guide* and newspaper files should be obtained as needed for reference.

Transparencies	2000 transparencies, plus a selection of subject matter masters
Other materials[1]	
Programed instructional materials	Printed, electronic, and other forms of programed materials
Realia	Models, dioramas, replicas, and other types of realia
Kits	
Art objects	
Video tape recordings	
Remote access programs	
Resource files	

Published by the American Library Association, *Chicago, Illinois* and the National Education Association, *Washington, D.C.*

School Staff

99

STANDARDS

AND

RECOMMENDATIONS

FOR

ELEMENTARY SCHOOLS

2. <u>Guidance Services</u> are essential for elementary children. It is during these formative years that identification of needs, prevention and correction of limiting behavior patterns, and stimulation for successful pursuits are most effective.

● Elementary children should have continuous assistance (1) to understand and to use wisely the potentialities they have and (2) to make use of the learning opportunities available.

● Each school should have an organized guidance program. It should provide the information and assistance necessary to aid the individual child in such areas as:
Transition from home to school and from elementary school to secondary school
Proper placement in the school program
Cumulative records
Counseling on individual problems
Referrals to community agencies for pupil-personnel problems
Planned standardized testing program

3. <u>Health Services</u> are important to the success of elementary children. The role of the school is to support the efforts of home and community in such areas as health education, disease control, safety, identification of health needs, and referrals to proper agencies.

● Schools should encourage use of available community health services.

● School health programs should provide such assisting services as:

Screening for health needs
Communicable disease control
Medical and dental clinics
Trained personnel to administer first aid
Special care for the handicapped
Health and safety education

● Trained personnel should be available to assist the school staff and to coordinate the health program. In some districts, this assistance may be arranged through the County Health Department.

STATE OF IDAHO
DEPARTMENT OF EDUCATION
BOISE, IDAHO

Authors' Note: The services for pupils such as the guidance program must be examined to see if they meet the state standards. The real benefit will accrue when the faculty looks for improvement in services above this narrow base. The needs of the pupils and the philosophy of the school will dominate in this review.

MINIMUM STANDARDS FOR NEW MEXICO SCHOOLS

STANDARDS FOR SPECIAL EDUCATION PROGRAMS

IV. Organization and Administration

A. The Special Education programs shall be a part of the regular
school program and housed in facilities which meet the particular needs of the children's exceptionalities.

B. Children shall be placed in Special Education classes according
to their dominant exceptionality. Mixed groups will be permitted
only where it can be shown that the program will benefit all
of the children.

E. The size of the class per teacher should not exceed 15 or be
less than 5. In the case of school systems having Special
Education programs where some Special Education children are
placed in selected regular classes, the ratio of the total
number of Special Education teachers in the system to the total
number of Special Education children should not exceed one
to 12. The same ratio shall apply in the case of cooperating
school systems served by an itinerant teacher. Exception may
be made for good cause upon approval of the State Superintendent of Public Instruction.

I. The ratio of specialist to children receiving Special Education services outside of the Special Education classroom or
the regular classroom shall be based upon the service
provided. The active case load of the speech and hearing
clinician, the psychologist and counselor providing
individual or small group clinical service should not
exceed 75 children at any one time. The resource or
supervisory teacher should work with no more than ten
Special Education classes, with adjustment being made for
individual situations. Exceptions may be made for good cause
upon approval by the State Superintendent of Public Instruction.

STATE OF NEW MEXICO
DEPARTMENT OF EDUCATION
SANTA FE

Authors' Note: The education of the special education pupils may or may not be a function of
the local elementary school. Many authorities wish to house special education children with the rest
of the typical children. If this is the situation then this aspect of the school program needs to be
carefully evaluated. The standards set by some states are similar to those of New Mexico.

GENERAL CONSIDERATIONS — SPECIAL EDUCATION STUDENTS

A child shall be considered handicapped under Chapter 46 of Title 18A when he is impaired physically, emotionally, intellectually or socially to such extent that without the aid of special facilities, special professional staff, special supplies and equipment, special time schedules and/or special methods of instruction he would not, in the judgment of the child study team, be expected to function educationally in a manner similar to that of children not so impaired. Determination that individual children are so handicapped and recommendation for appropriate program and/or placement shall be the function of the basic child study team employed by a local board of education.

A basic child study team, acting in consultation with a physician, shall consist of a school psychologist, a learning disabilities specialist, and a school social worker. A child study team may also include a psychiatrist experienced in work with children, a school administrator, a classroom teacher, a school nurse, a guidance counselor, a speech correctionist, a remedial reading teacher, and other members of the school professional staff as may be recommended by the basic child study team with the approval of the chief school administrator. Specific professional personnel as described in these rules and regulations are required in the classification of certain handicaps and their reports shall be considered by the basic child study team in making those certain classifications. A comprehensive physical examination shall be given by a physician (see Section III., B 1.).

All children classified shall have such classification established during a conference attended by a representative of each of the basic professional areas and such classification shall be based on the data obtained by the prescribed professionals.

All members of the basic child study team shall be employees of the board of education or the State Board of Education. Approval of the Commissioner of Education shall be obtained for the purchase by the local school district of services of eligible and/or approved diagnostic clinics, agencies, or professionals in private practice representing a basic child study team discipline functioning in lieu of or to supplement members of the basic child study team.

Classification shall be used to plan appropriate educational programs, to determine and to provide appropriate facilities and to provide a basis for the assignment of the appropriately qualified instructional staff. Effort shall be made by the local district to prevent needless public labeling or categorizing classified children.

Reports submitted by local school districts to the Bureau of Special Education and Pupil Personnel Services shall be sent via the office of the respective county superintendent.

Division of Curriculum and Instruction
Bureau of Special Education and Pupil
Personnel Services

New Jersey State Dept.
of Education
Trenton, New Jersey

Author's Note: The regulations of the State Departments of Education amplify, clarify, and specify general policies of the state. In these administration regulations the real purpose of the policy is implemented. New Jersey regulations are exemplary in this regard in respect to the education of the special education children.

The Elementary School Guide

THE ELEMENTARY TEACHER

Statement of Guiding Principles

A school can be no better than the individual teachers who make up its faculty. Yet, a staff of well-qualified teachers do not insure a good school. The teachers within a system must work as part of the overall team which is composed of the superintendent, supervisors, principal, librarians, teachers, secretaries, custodians, bus drivers, cafeteria workers, and other school employees.

Teachers must continue to grow personally, academically, and professionally.

The teacher's primary responsibility is to give instruction but his work goes farther than this since he is helping develop future citizens. The teacher will not only teach the basic curriculum, he will inspire and motivate each pupil helping him to discover and develop his full potential.

III. RELATIONSHIPS WITH PUPILS

E S N L 1. The teacher is acutely aware of individual differences in children.

E S N L 2. The teacher does not expect the same achievement from all his pupils and recognizes that a uniform standard for all is unrealistic.

E S N L 3. The teacher tries to explore and develop the talents of each pupil.

E S N L 4. The teacher encourages the pupils to recognize the good qualities in pupils and to appreciate the unique contribution each person makes to the group and to his country.

E S N L 5. The teacher and pupils participate in varied activities which provide for democratic experiences in the classroom.

E S N L 6. The teacher helps each pupil to grow in self-control and self-direction.

E S N L 7. The teacher is aware of the needs created by the social environment in which pupils live.

E S N L 8. The teacher helps each pupil feel that he is needed and wanted.

E S N L 9. The teacher provides ways and means for each pupil to contribute to the activities of the class.

E S N L 10. The teacher provides opportunities for pupils to participate in planning activities.

E S N L 11. The teacher holds the pupils responsible for completion of work started and provides the necessary time.

E S N L 12. The teacher provides opportunities for all pupils to develop skill as a leader and as a follower.

E S N L 13. The teacher evaluates each pupil's progress with reference to his individual growth pattern.

E S N L 14. The teacher helps the pupil to become aware of his progress.

E S N L 15. The teacher avoids personal domination, ridicule, sarcasm, and other negative methods of control.

continued

Authors' Note: Teacher-pupil relationships have always been a significant part of the elementary school evaluation. No evaluation can be truly complete unless this area is fully covered in the criteria. The philosophy of the school and this relationship are critically bound together and must reflect this relationship.

ESNL 16. Children with physical defects are given proper consideration and encouraged to participate to the fullest extent of his ability.

ESNL 17. The teacher provides for each pupil an opportunity to participate in group games and leisure activities that contribute to optimum physical development.

ESNL 18. The teacher provides rest periods at regular times for pupils as needed.

ESNL 19. The teacher keeps a cumulative record of each pupil.

ESNL 20. The pupil's cumulative records follow him from year to year.

ESNL 21. The teacher provides a permanent health record for each pupil.

ESNL 22. The teacher considers pupil placement on the basis of need and readiness for learning, considering the mental, physical, emotional, and social maturity of the child.

ESNL 23. The teacher, through example, helps the pupils to become tolerant of all people and to appreciate the contributions to society that each has made.

ESNL 24. The teacher helps pupils to appreciate their aesthetic surroundings.

State Department of Education
Little Rock, Arkansas

THE PERFORMANCE OF TEACHERS AND PUPILS IN SMALL CLASSES

IDENTIFYING SUPERIOR TEACHERS

In its work, the Commission on the 1980 School made considerable use of the Central School Study's *Identifying Superior Teachers*,[3] as well as of extensive work in individual communities of the Metropolitan School Study Council. From these sources, the Commission established a "Compendium of Superior Teacher Characteristics." This compendium is composed of 12 major qualities of a superior teacher:

1. Should have a thorough background balanced between the liberal arts and methods of teaching.

2. Possess knowledge in breadth and depth in his area of specialization.

3. Is aware of the potential values inherent in mass education, and therefore is not opposed to it, but retains an abiding interest in the individual student.

4. Is conscious of the need to develop the potential of each pupil.

5. Establishes a positive relationship between himself and his charges.

6. Uses diverse methods to challenge his students constantly.

7. Welcomes professional evaluation by conscientious educators.

8. Is an active participant in professional organizations.

9. Keeps the parents of his children well informed and is interested in maintaining favorable school-community relations.

10. Is interested in and familiar with education developments beyond the limits of his classroom, his school, and his school system.

11. Wishes to play an active part in efforts directed towards improving the quality of American education.

12. Is aware of the neccessity for harmonious teacher-teacher and teacher-administrator relationships and seeks out ways in which to establish and maintain such relationships.

[2]Paul R. Mort, "Progress Report on the School of 1980," (New York: Institute of Administrative Research, Teachers' College, Columbia University, 1961), pp. 13-16 (Mimeographed)

[3]Central School Boards Committee for Educational Research, *Identifying Superior Teachers* (New York: Institute of Administrative Research, Teachers College, Columbia University, 1959).

[4]Matthew W. Gaffney, "A Compendium of Superior Teacher Characteristics" (New York: Metropolitan School Study Council, Teachers College, Columbia University, 1961). (Mimeographed).

James B. Pugh
Research Associate, Institute of Administrative Research
Teachers College, Columbia University

Metropolitan School Study Council

Commission on the School of 1980
Commission Study No. 1

Institute of Administrative Research
Teachers College, Columbia University

Authors' Note: The evaluating of teachers is a topic that most evaluation criteria skip because it is too "hot"—too "threatening" for the faculty to consider. The example suggests that when there are small classes there should be resultant changes in the performance of the teacher. Since these are not related to an individual teacher, and since there is no "grade" or salary connection, the faculty should be able to really focus on this item.

PHILOSOPHY OF TEACHER EVALUATION

One of the most important obligations of the teaching profession is the development and implementation of an instructional program that meets realistic, societal needs of boys and girls. Personnel who can carry out these responsibilities must be employed. Some type of evaluation becomes a necessary part of the instructional program to make certain that the performance of the personnel is meeting the expected goals of the instructional program.

The following assumptions are inherent in this philosophy of teacher evaluation:

1. Evaluation begins with the acceptance of a teaching contract and does not end until a teacher leaves the school district. This presupposes self-evaluation as well as evaluation by members of the administrative staff.

2. Evaluation is a process of linking together the educational goals of the school system and the performance of the teacher. This assumes that there must be active participation in the evaluation by both the evaluator and the person being evaluated.

3. The desired outcome of teacher evaluation should always be increased effectiveness of personnel in improving the instructional program.

Therefore, evaluation of teaching in the Caldwell-West Caldwell Schools shall be a continuing process designed to help teachers and administrators carry out the prescribed school philosophy and curriculum for the benefit of all students in the school district.

CALDWELL-WEST CALDWELL SCHOOLS
Caldwell, New Jersey

continued

Authors' Note: The example states a basic philosophy for teacher evaluation with definite procedures to carry out the program. This is one of the contentious items of teacher-administration conflict. Precise and clear directions will assist in carrying out the vital administration duty.

INSTRUCTIONS FOR EVALUATION PROCESS

The attached Professional Evaluation Guide Sheets are to be used as a guide in the evaluation of teachers. The actual evaluation shall be in narrative form signed by both the principal and the teacher.

A. <u>Non-Tenure</u>   Part I of the evaluation form (Teachers in the Classroom) shall be completed by the building principal two or more times per year for non-tenure professional personnel. Parts II, III, and IV shall be completed by the building principal at least once annually.

B. <u>Tenure</u>   Part I shall be completed by the building principal on tenure personnel at least once a year. Parts II, III, and IV shall be completed by the building principal at least once every two years.

C. Preliminary materials may be furnished by the teacher to the evaluator such as: purposes of lesson, method employed, homework, lesson plans, etc.

D. Total evaluation of all professional personnel is to be on the basis of the team approach involving the Superintendent, Assistant Superintendent, Building Principals, and any other supervisory personnel so designated. It shall be the responsibility of the Superintendent of Schools to make final recommendations to Board of Education.

E. After each evaluation is completed on the narrative form, the evaluator shall discuss the results with the person being evaluated.

F. Copies of the completed evaluation form shall be placed on file in the Superintendent's office and a carbon copy given the teacher being evaluated for his personal record.

G. The non-tenure teacher shall be notified of at least one scheduled evaluation visit a year at a time agreeable to both parties.

I.   THE TEACHER IN THE CLASSROOM

II.   THE TEACHER AS A PERSON

III. THE TEACHER AS A MEMBER OF THE PROFESSION

IV. THE TEACHER WITH PARENTS AND COMMUNITY

Caldwell-West Caldwell Public Schools
Caldwell, New Jersey

PROVIDING FACILITIES FOR PHYSICAL DEVELOPMENT

The nature of any program will be affected by the adequacy of the facilities available for its operation. Programs which have as their primary purpose the formation of skills and habits conducive to health, safety, and physical development need special facilities to make them effective.

The importance of good physical development and health contribute not only to the child as an individual but to our needs as a nation. It is a vital program and should receive the support it needs to successfully accomplish its purposes.

We therefore recognize as an objective of the Learning Environment — the provision of facilities which permit a well-rounded program in the areas of physical education, health, and safety.

CHECK (√) ONE

To a High Degree	To Some Degree	Not At All	Unable To Evaluate	TO WHAT DEGREE DO EACH OF THE FOLLOWING PRACTICES AND CONDITIONS EXIST IN OUR SCHOOL?
				1. The gymnasium or indoor activity area is large enough to meet the needs of the program. Comments:
				2. The gymnasium or indoor activity area is well-lighted and ventilated. Comments:
				3. A suitable variety of gymnastic apparatus is available. Comments:
				4. The gymnasium floor is lined clearly for games used in the developmental physical education program. Comments:
				5. Equipment is readily available for use in the sports program of the school. Comments:
				6. Storage space for equipment is adequate and conveniently located. Comments:
				7. Locker rooms and showers are sufficient in number and maintained in a clean, healthful manner. Comments:
				8. The outdoor recreation area is large enough to permit the activities of the program to function. Comments:
				9. The play area is in a suitable location away from classrooms. Comments:

New Jersey School Development Council - Graduate School of Education, Rutgers - The State University, New Brunswick, N. J.

Authors' Note: The evaluation of the physical facilities is one of the easier tasks for the local committee to perform. Most state departments of education have suggested standards. In addition the national professional organizations publish recommendations for the physical and utilization standards of most of the special rooms in the school, such as the gymnasium, the library, the art room.

SCHOOLHOUSE PLANNING
and
CONSTRUCTION

202
ELEMENTARY SCHOOLS

202.1   Classrooms

Most elementary schools are planned around a classroom which is designed to contain or facilitate almost all normal classroom activities of the pupils in the area. Considerable attention needs to be given, therefore, to the design of these rooms. Each instructional area should be provided with the following types of equipment: student wardrobe (unless corridor lockers are used), teacher's wardrobe, filing cabinet, storage cabinets, book shelves and/or carts, sink cabinet with drinking fountain, work counters, and movable classroom furniture of various types which will facilitate both individual and group work. Special equipment is also desirable for specially planned areas such as library, arts, science, and music centers. Equipment should be so located as never to impede safe exit from the room.

The amount of chalkboard and tackboard in each room should vary depending on the grade level and the instructional methods used.

All rooms should be equipped for the use of visual and auditory aids with adequate electric outlets, room darkening devices, projection screens, and map display rails.

There is little agreement on the question of which storage units should be built-in and which should be portable. There seems to be some merit, however, in being able to move storage units about the room to form temporary partially divided areas for special individual or group activities, and it is likely that these activities will increase in future years

601
INSTRUCTIONAL ROOMS

601.1   Area

601.1a   Every instructional room area shall be planned in consideration of the number of pupils to be housed, the program of instruction to be followed, and the educational purposes of the room.

601.1b   It is recommended that standard classrooms be planned in accordance with the following table:

T A B L E I
Instructional Areas

Grade or Subject	Desirable	Acceptable
Kindergarten	1,200 sq. ft.	900 sq. ft.
Grades 1 to 3	1,000 sq. ft.	800 sq. ft.
4 to 8	900 sq. ft.	700 sq. ft.
9 to 12	800 sq. ft.	650 sq. ft.

601.1c   Space recommendations for other instructional areas are indicated in special bulletins available from the Director of School Planning Service.

State of New Jersey   **Department of Education**

Trenton

Authors' Note: The example illustrates state department of education recommendations for instructional areas. This is one of the easier items to assess as to the meeting of standards. The opinion of the faculty on these items is critical for faculty morale. It is also of great help if a building program is being contemplated.

School-Community Relations

O S S T F

P U B L I C   R E L A T I O N S

H A N D B O O K

Published by THE PUBLIC RELATIONS

DEPARTMENT, ONTARIO SECONDARY

SCHOOL TEACHERS' FEDERATION,

FEDERATION HOUSE,

1260 BAY STREET,

TORONTO 5, ONTARIO.

STUDENTS

The experienced teacher is likely to believe—and quite rightly—that a good job of teaching is the best kind of public relations, whether with students or any other section of the public. The mature and successful teacher—the teacher who knows his subject, is consistent and impartial in discipline, refrains from sarcasm, and recognizes the needs and rights of students—is the profession's number one public relations man or woman.

Additionally, however, the good teacher should build good relations with students by participation in at least one extra-curricular activity that brings him into a more informal relationship with a smaller group of students.

Insofar as the teacher can treat the high school student as a young adult rather than as an overgrown child, so much will teacher-student relations be improved.

Here are 19 ways to build good student relations:
— Maintain the best possible state of mental and physical health
— Refrain from the use of sarcasm, ridicule and other unworthy devices
— Give evidence of emotional maturity and stability
— Be consistent in class management and discipline
— Treat all students imparially, regardless of social and family backgrounds
— Maintain a sense of humour
— Don't carry a grudge against any student
— Refuse to join with other staff members in taking concerted prejudicial action against a student
— Abstain from unfavourable comparison of a student with other members of his family who are, or have been, in attendance at the school
— Try to maintain conditions in the classroom that will best assist the student in the learning process
— Recognize each student's individuality and rights
— Respect the opinions of students, even though they may differ from yours
— Be enthusiastic about the importance and presentation of the subjects on the curriculum
— Acknowledge in a gracious manner any errors, oversights or misjudgments affecting the students
— Continue your own learning procedure, thus associating yourself with your students as learners
— Know your own and related subjects thoroughly
— Make due allowances for special circumstances in a student's environment or physical condition which may have an effect on his school achievements or attitude
— Show a personal concern for the student's interests and activities, even beyond those of the classroom
— Exemplify day by day the essential characteristics of good citizenship

Authors' Note: This is a most unusual policy. In public relations the normal emphasis is on the relationship between the school and the teacher, parent, general public. The student relationship is neglected and ignored; and this statement by our Canadian neighbors of the importance of this concept is most relevant. This is particularly so when student unrest is so prevalent.

Standards
of
Mississippi
Accrediting
Commission

III. Public Relations

The administrator should employ democratic procedures in all relations with the public, the faculty, the students, and the board of trustees. This involves supplying accurate information concerning both deficiencies and progress of the school as a basis for obtaining cooperative endeavor from all groups to meet the needs of the children of the school. Such devices as yearly reports, publications, contacts with community organizations, newspaper publicity, citizens' advisory committees, and personal conferences may be used.

Standards For Accrediting Public And Private Elementary And Secondary Schools

---

Authors' Note: Many states are now stressing, and in many cases recommending, that the individual school district take positive steps to have an on-going program of public relations. For the individual elementary school this is a natural process, accepted as a responsibility, and eagerly evaluated.

objectives for school public relations

the role of the local association

The role of the local education association in interpreting the schools to the public can tip the balance in favor of adequate support for schools.

The Committee on Public Relations for the PSEA has adopted basic objectives which are readily adaptable to the local association program. The Committee urges local associations to set goals comparable to those adopted by the Committee and approved by the PSEA Executive Council in 1960. These goals are as follows:

SUGGESTED GOALS FOR A LOCAL PUBLIC RELATIONS COMMITTEE

—to provide periodically ideas to stimulate activity on the local level

—to cooperate in the promotion of convocations geared to the educational needs of the region or local areas

—to promote intercommittee action

—to assist other committees in the local association and in the community by interpreting their programs and projects to the membership and to the public

We seek public understanding that today's schools and teachers continue to recognize and emphasize the importance of the fundamentals of learning.

We seek public understanding that the first concern and deepest interest of teachers lie in what is best for our children.

We seek public understanding that every citizen in Pennsylvania has an inescapable responsibility for providing, maintaining and financing the best schools and teachers.

We seek to achieve common goals through interrelationship activities with PSEA Committees on the state and local levels.

PICK A PR CHAIRMAN

—with a knack of working with people

—with a journalistic flair

—with promotional talent

—with ability to dig out news

—with a sense for feature material

—with a bit of showmanship

—with a desire to lead a committee

—with ability to build contacts and relationships with city officials, civic leaders and news outlets

**PENNSYLVANIA STATE EDUCATION ASSOCIATION
400 NORTH THIRD STREET, HARRISBURG, PENNSYLVANIA**

Authors' Note: The teacher association may not have a role in the evaluation process, but many of the objectives listed for the association can be readily adapted for the local school.

3

Viewing Ourselves:
The Self-Evaluation Process

Make it thy business to know thyself,
which is the most difficult lesson in the world.
—Cervantes, *Don Quixote*

The self-evaluation experience may well be the most important aspect of the entire assessment procedure for the school district. This chapter will address itself to the practical aspects of conducting a self-evaluation of all of the elementary units of a school system. Discussed will be how this whole self-assessment activity flows from idea to reality.

HOW TO PROCEED

Obviously, leadership must be provided for such an enterprise. Decisions need to be made concerning who these key people will be and how they will be selected. Also, their responsibilities ought to be clearly stated. Total involvement of the staff requires that they be well organized into functioning work groups that are efficient and productive. The kinds of groups, their composition and their duties all have to be spelled out. Suggested here are two types of units, the coordinating committee and the specific self-study group. These groups, established for introspective study, need tactful guidance in how best to employ methods of gathering data. Timetables should be agreed upon in advance of the study. Decisions should also be reached concerning such issues as early pupil dismissal and released time for teachers. The great culminating activity, the preparation of the final self-evaluation report, must be done with careful coordination of content and format. Only then will the district be able to say that it has looked within itself for "what is" and "what should be" and is now ready for confirmation or denial of the findings from a visiting team of evaluators.

IDEA ORIGIN

The idea to have the elementary schools evaluate themselves could originate from a variety of sources. The principal may ask for it. Citizens organized into P.T.A.'s or

Better School Associations may request an overview of their schools. It may be that the Board of Education wishes an appraisal of the schools and charges the school administrators with the responsibility for carrying it out. Most likely the chief school executive will approach his administrative colleagues and the Board of Education to ascertain interest in such a project. Failure to secure this coordination would jeopardize the entire project. Approval and cooperation of each is highly desirable.

CHAIRMAN APPOINTED

Once the idea takes hold, the question arises as to the best kind of organizational pattern conducive to self-evaluation. It is here that the superintendent of schools must begin the process by selecting a chairman. This most vital position usually would come from the administrative echelon, i.e., elementary principal, assistant superintendent or director of instruction. While there may be a teacher who is very qualified for the role, it must be remembered that sufficient released time will need to be granted this person in order to provide him with adequate opportunities for the work to be accomplished.

CHAIRMAN'S RESPONSIBILITIES

The newly appointed chairman should be oriented by the superintendent concerning the specific responsibilities of the position. They are as follows:
1. Provide leadership to the total self-evaluation procedure. Be responsible for the success of the entire enterprise.
2. With the superintendent, seek out and invite the best qualified representatives of each school to serve on the Coordinating Committee. Building principals' advice may also be sought concerning their most able personnel.
3. Conduct the regular sessions of the Coordinating Committee. Appoint a recorder for the compilation of data resulting from the group's work.
4. Join work-study group sessions frequently to provide consultation and inspiration. Visiting personnel during their work sessions will demonstrate the chairman's deep interest in all facets of the study.
5. Provide the district's administrative and teaching staff with regular progress reports of the self-evaluation. Presented monthly, these are essential in keeping the system's leaders knowledgeable and equipped to handle any questions arising from teachers and parents.
6. Be prepared to report directly to the Board of Education. If the Superintendent prefers to do this himself, it still will be the responsibility of the chairman to submit the self-evaluative progress information required for the Board.

COMPOSITION OF COORDINATING COMMITTEE

Establishing the Coordinating Committee will be one of the first things the Superintendent and his new chairman will do. Names of capable personnel can be obtained by consultation with the other administrators. It is desirable to have each elementary school represented so that the committee has the benefit of each building staff's thoughts. The faculty of each can thus be kept informed by one of their own concerning the self-evaluation's progress. If there are as few as four schools, it may be wise to have two representatives from each school. When one school is considerably larger than others, that building may have its representation increased. When selecting teachers, it is advantageous for a balanced representation to have them come from different grade levels. If two teachers are from one building, one ought to be from the primary grades and the other from the intermediate level. An attempt might be made to have the coordinating committee have at least one member from each of the grades of the elementary school organization.

OTHER POSSIBILITIES FOR COMMITTEE

Other positions may be represented on the Coordinating Committee. Selection may be made from the following:

1. Principals—An elementary school principal can adequately represent the views of his colleagues and contribute much from his vantage point as head of a school.
2. Special service personnel—Psychologists, social workers, learning disabilities specialists, speech therapists, etc., represent a view of elementary education from the standpoint of their orientation to child study.
3. Teacher specialists—Those working as specialists in reading, mathematics, science, music, physical education, and art may contribute toward the committee's work by representing a depth understanding of a specific subject area.
4. Board of Education member—It may be desired that a Board of Education member act as a liaison between the Board and the Coordinating Committee. If this direct representation is not desired, then an alternate suggestion is to have a former Board member join the Committee. Knowledge of Board and community activities is obviously the strength that he can bring to the group's efforts.
5. P.T.A. member—When a district has a composite or federate P.T.A. organization, this representative may be one of that group's officers. Lacking this, a school system may, of course, select from any one of their individual school P.T.A.'s.
6. Teacher organization member—Some may deem it a positive step to include a representative from the district's teacher organization. This person can reflect the views of this unit which has been established as a collective spokesman for the school system's teachers.
7. Secondary school teacher—In order to enhance the articulation of elementary and secondary schools, the presence of a junior or senior high school teacher may be valuable to the Committee.
8. Administrative interns—Both for the contribution this person can make and for the value of the experience for him, it is possible for the administrative trainee to be included.
9. Non-professional employees—Secretaries, clerks, custodians, maintenance men and cafeteria workers could be represented on this Committee or in specific self-study groups. Particular contributions can be made by these employees when areas are evaluated that involve their day-to-day responsibilities.
10. The Superintendent—It would be expected that the system's chief executive may join, as time permits, any of the activities of the Coordinating Committee.

SIZE OF COMMITTEE

What then should be the size of the Coordinating Committee? Must all of the positions listed above be included? Each school system planning a self-evaluation must make such decisions. Committees can be successful in achieving their purposes whether they have five or fifteen members. Usually more than fifteen becomes somewhat unwieldy. To be stressed are the principles of adequate representation from all categories of positions and equitable delegation from all grade and subject areas.

INVITATION TO PARTICIPATE

An individual invitation to participate sent to each prospective member of the Coordinating Committee signed by both the superintendent and the chairman of the self-evaluation offers the best chance of being well received by the persons selected.

SAMPLE INVITATION LETTER

Below is a sample of an Invitational Letter to Prospective Members of the Coordinating Committee.

Dear Mr. _____ :

It is with considerable enthusiasm that we are planning a complete self-evaluation of our elementary schools. We're sure you will agree with us and our Board of Education that the value of such a project will be tremendous. It is expected that total staff involvement in this self-appraisal will result in action benefiting the education of every youngster in all of our elementary classes. The key direction to be given this important project will come from the Coordinating Committee. This group, comprised of a cross-section of administrators, teachers, and specialists, will work closely with us to guide our assessment of ourselves throughout the coming year. We would be particularly pleased if you would join the group.

Your representation of the area of endeavor in which you have proven yourself is important to the success of the project. Don't hesitate to contact either of us concerning our desire to have you as a member of the Coordinating Committee.

Sincerely,

_____ Superintendent
_____ Chairman, Self-
Evaluation

FUNCTIONS OF THE COORDINATING COMMITTEE

The superintendent and the chairman of the self-evaluation will want to make their charge to the Coordinating Committee very clear at the first meeting.

Basic responsibilities of the Coordinating Committee are:

1. Select evaluation criteria. A thorough review of Chapter 2 of this volume will provide the group with the insight required before selecting an evaluation instrument. The matching of criteria to the school system's philosophy is of basic importance. Adaptation is usually required of an existing instrument in order that it meet such local situations as grade organization, curriculum differences or unique physical plants.

2. Establish a self-evaluation timetable. Crucial to the entire enterprise are guidelines of time. How long shall the study take? How frequently shall the working groups meet? When shall they meet? The Coordinating Committee needs to resolve these questions. Discussion of solutions will be treated later in this chapter.

3. List charges to be made to the specific self-study groups. All personnel should be involved in these working groups. Their responsibilities must be carefully outlined for their guidance by the Coordinating Committee.

4. Decide on the most advantageous work areas for the various study groups. The best places are well-lighted, comfortable, seldom interrupted and easily reached by all. Ideally, classrooms should be avoided in favor of rooms with a conference table and chairs that can stand the test of being comfortable for a long session. Faculty rooms, libraries, conference areas and some offices lend themselves to these requirements.

5. Produce regular progress reports of the self-evaluation. It is vital to the cohesiveness of the working groups that they be frequently apprised of the progress other groups are making. Morale suffers if each group works in such isolation that it does not feel part of the total effort. In addition to total staff meetings within the duration of the self-evaluation, a staff newsletter can be utilized to keep all school personnel informed. Through the chairman and the superintendent, reports should be made to the administrative staff and to the Board of Education.

6. Prepare material for the local news media. It is important to keep the citizens of the community aware of the self-evaluation process. Examination of their schools is accepted as a welcome activity by most communities. Recommendations coming forth will be supported more fully if they are not the first evidence the public has of the assessment procedure. Often one member of the committee is assigned to act as a regular liaison to newspapers, radio and TV.

7. Develop the self-evaluation final report. This will be the tangible evidence of hours of work by many dedicated people. The form it shall take, the sequence of content, and a review of all submitted data will be the major responsibility of the Coordinating Committee. Suggestions for its preparation will be developed later in this chapter.

SPECIFIC SELF-STUDY GROUPS

The specific self-study groups are created and charged with responsibilities by the Coordinating Committee. The areas that these working teams would cover must match the evaluative criteria instrument. Decisions of what is to be evaluated as discussed in Chapter 1 would influence the choice of evaluative criteria which, in turn, mandates the areas requiring specific study. Usual categories involved in a full self-evaluation would include:

1. School Physical Plant
2. Instructional Equipment

3. School Personnel
4. Administration and Supervision
5. Pupil Personnel Services
6. Home-School-Community Relations
7. Library Services
8. School Philosophy
9. Curricular Areas
    a) Art
    b) Kindergarten
    c) Language Arts
    d) Mathematics
    e) Music
    f) Physical Education
    g) Science
    h) Social Studies

Each district undergoing a self-evaluation would vary in its requirements for areas to be covered. For instance, there may be a desire to emphasize Reading by separating that subject from the Language Arts. On the other hand, Art and Music could be combined as "The Arts" and be studied by one group.

COMPOSITION OF SPECIFIC SELF-STUDY GROUPS

The membership of the specific self-study groups is based on total involvement of the entire professional staff. Every teacher should be able to have the opportunity of being a direct inquirer into at least one facet of the school system. Each study group would contain:

1 member of coordinating committee
1-2 administrative or supervisory personnel
1-6 teachers
1-4 persons directly related to area of study

It is beneficial if the coordinating committee has at least one representative on each self study group. This permits communication to flow in both directions between the specific inquiring units and the Coordinating Committee. It is well to have administrative and supervisory personnel in each group because of their ability to bring forth information based on a wider scope of orientation than is possible for the classroom teacher. The number of teachers within each unit will vary according to the size of the district's faculty. An attempt should be made to have teacher representation from each school spread throughout all the committees rather than permitting them to cluster in any one study area. Also advantageous is to have delegates from a variety of grade levels included in each section. In this way, a balanced appraisal can be carried through by the presence of staff from different vantage points. In the larger school districts, there may be enough teachers so that the study group comprises representatives from each grade. Smaller systems may have one primary and one intermediate teacher in each group.

TEACHER SPECIALISTS ON COMMITTEE

Important in each specific self-study group should be one or more members who are particularly related to the area under inquiry. As an example, the music specialist would be included in the music unit, the superintendent of buildings in the school physical plant section and a P.T.A. officer might be part of the home-school-community relations section. Their direct knowledge is invaluable to studies relative to their point of reference.

It is expected that the Superintendent of Schools and the Director of the self-evaluation would have an open invitation to visit any study group at any time. Their presence and experience will contribute to the success of the enterprise.

SELECTION OF CHAIRMAN, RECORDER OF SELF-STUDY GROUPS

The chairman of each self-study section is best elected by the group at its first meeting. With success largely based on how well the members work with each other, it is wise to have the leadership be of their own choosing. Some units may wish to rotate the chairmanship in order to share this duty. In any event, the chairman should select a recorder so that each meeting's accomplishments are properly accounted for. Further, these notes will be helpful to the chairman or the representative of the Coordinating Committee when reports are made to that parent body.

FUNCTIONS OF SPECIFIC SELF-STUDY GROUPS

The functions of the specific self-study groups may be divided into four parts: 1. Gathering data, 2. Fulfilling the evaluation instrument's requirements, 3. Making recommendations, and 4. Reporting to the Coordinating Committee.

WAYS OF COLLECTING DATA

The task of collecting the data provides each group member with opportunities for active participation. This process frequently takes various forms.

1. Inspection Tours—For example, the group studying the School Physical Plant would set out to visit each building. Judgments would be made in line with the evaluative criteria with both satisfactory and unsatisfactory items noted. Usually it is best to tour each school accompanied by the principal and head custodian. Both are vital in pointing out information required and facts that are unique to that individual building. Making recommendations concerning the physical plant are abetted by tours of neighboring district's schools especially those of recent vintage or having notable innovation.

2. Taking inventory—An analysis of a district's adequacy of instructional equipment and supplies requires the facts concerning quantity and quality. Inventories exist and are available in most areas, but inventories alone do not give adequate information concerning the quality, utilization, or distribution of the equipment and supplies. Investigation must be

made into the details supporting and supplementing the inventory. Audio-visual equipment, for example, would not be noted only for its presence, but for the method of distribution to the classroom teacher. Inquiries would also be made about the methods employed to order teaching aids.

3. Interviewing—A careful scrutiny of any evaluative criteria will reveal that information is required that is best gained by asking people directly related to the area. When studying Personnel, Administration, or Pupil Services, for instance, it is appropriate to first formulate an interview guide outlining questions that need to be asked of certain personnel. Then one or two group members would see and speak to the people who are routinely performing the tasks that are being studied. Principals, supervisors, specialists, psychologists and teachers may be questioned relative to the "whys," "whats" and "hows" of their respective disciplines. For the benefit of reporting back to the group, a tape recorder would be invaluable in permitting effective sharing of the elicited information.

4. Surveying via questionnaires—Committees may wish to secure responses from a group of people to ascertain the facts within a certain category. When the task requires answers from the faculty of a school or each of the kindergarten teachers, the interview technique may be too time consuming. A written questionnaire can be prepared in order to seek out current practices from numbers of personnel. This device also often affords an insight into the needs of a group, i.e., teachers, who may desire certain changes in the science curriculum or increased use of library services.

5. Visiting other school systems—There is value in seeing what others do. Observing classes elsewhere enables contrasts or similarities to come into focus. Hearing administrative procedures related from another district provides food for thought as to what is being done at home and can point the direction towards that which should be done. As mentioned above, physical plant comparisons can also lead to decisions about the status of present buildings and needs for the future.

6. Engaging outside consultants—It may be considered helpful to a specific study group's work to arrange for a visit from a recognized authority in the group's field of inquiry. A nearby college or university may provide an outstanding scholar in reading education, an expert of library resource centers or a music educator of considerable renown. When studying community relations, it could be appropriate to listen to the thoughts of a public relations expert. The authority may sit in on several of the group's sessions making pertinent contributions or he might be called in for a more formal presentation to the group where he provides them with the benefit of his training and experience.

FULFILLING THE EVALUATION INSTRUMENT'S REQUIREMENTS

Another important function of the specific self-study groups is to fulfill the requirements of the evaluative instrument criteria which has been selected. As was seen in Chapter 2, format of evaluation publications do differ and each has its own guidelines for most effective use. All require, however, indications from each study group about present policies and current practices related to their area of inquiry. Often it is appropriate to include additional practices or conditions which exist in the district that contribute to the subject being investigated. As this is being accomplished it will be evident how the communication of ideas among the committee members becomes an extremely valuable aspect of the entire project. The in-service growth of professional staff is an important outcome of the sessions where the facts concerning the district's procedures are matched against the evaluative criteria being used.

MAKING RECOMMENDATIONS

Frequently considered the most vital aspect of the work of the self-study group is the making of recommendations for future improvement within the scope of the topic they have scrutinized. When the gathering of the data is accomplished and the facts reveal the extent to which the objective in the criteria is being met, it will be obvious that some practices or conditions need improvement. The judgment of the group should bring forth definite recommendations. For instance, knowledge of the value of a recent change in spelling instruction cannot be measured until testing is administered after a period of a year. The study group would recommend when testing should be done, to whom, and offer suggestions about the way to do it. Further, it may be decided that certain practices are outmoded and need revision. Perhaps entirely new ideas will enhance the instruction in, let us say, music. Recommendations might be made such as asking for preparation of a list of parents who have unique musical talents to visit classrooms, explain their specialty and musically demonstrate the features of the instrument.

If the study group feels that additional personnel may bolster an area of study within the district, it may list a recommendation such as a request for a science specialist to develop the program, coordinate the use of equipment and facilities and to act as a resource person in science for the classroom teacher.

The physical dimension may call for recommendations to increase library facilities, provide more storage areas, add bulletin boards, or install audio-visual darkening draperies.

REPORTING TO THE COORDINATING COMMITTEE

Fortified by completion of the requirements of the instrument of evaluative criteria and the listing of appropriate recommendations, the self-study group has now only to make its report to the Coordinating Committee. This will include the completed evaluative instrument usually with ratings, graphs, tables, or other items required by the format. In addition, comments should be offered that are pertinent to the data and are best made clear via a narrative explanation. Appropriate samples can be submitted such as test results, suggested book recommendations or copies of articles written by experts in the field. Without fail, the recommendations of the group should be attached to its report that goes to the parent unit. These, with the completed evaluation instrument, additional comments and samples of pertinent value will comprise the body of information to be submitted at the conclusion of the study group's investigation.

SELF-EVALUATION TIMETABLE

Essential to the progress of the self-evaluation project is a pre-determined schedule for all the necessary activities. This timetable can be planned initially by the Superintendent and the self-evaluation Chairman, and then submitted to the Coordinating Committee for its review. This group, representing all schools and categories of positions should have the opportunity to approve the routine that they and their counterparts will be following during the system's self-appraisal. Whenever the normal length of the school day is modified in any way for the self-evaluation project, it is necessary that the Board of Education give its permission. Also, if there is going to be any released time for teachers, it is conceivable that a discussion of these hours would be held with the teachers organization. In some districts, this would take the form of negotiations and result in a written agreement.

SUMMER MEETINGS

One year will be required for an adequate treatment of a school district's self-evaluation. Although a child's school year typically runs from September to June, it would be well for the superintendent not to wait for the opening of the new school year before he selects his self-evaluation chairman. With a chairman chosen in May, the business of selecting members of the Coordinating Committee can commence immediately. With this group chosen before the school year end, it may be possible to arrange for summer meetings.

The advantage of having personnel free from their regular duties in order to devote their full effort to the task at hand is obvious. As little as one or two weeks of regular meetings can accomplish more than months of intermittent gatherings during the regular school year. If it is not possible to have the entire Coordinating Committee meet then, it would still be very beneficial to have a sub-committee assigned to seeking out the most appropriate evaluative criteria for the district. After this small group's analysis of existing instruments, the total committee will be better able to make a decision. This important phase must be accomplished before the specific self-study groups are formed. The Board of Education and the teacher organization will both have an interest in any summer work planned for personnel involved in the self-study. Here again agreements need be reached concerning salaries and time on the job.

The first gathering of all of the school system's staff directly concerned with the self-evaluation should be held in early October. Quite appropriate on this occasion is an explanation of the benefits of evaluation (see Chapter 1) by the Superintendent or an invited consultant knowledgeable in the field. The President of the Board of Education may also at this time display his group's support for the project by speaking to the assembled about the Board's reasons for backing the evaluative process. The Chairman of the self-evaluation is best prepared to outline the steps taken thus far and to indicate the procedures to be followed in the coming year. The first meetings of the specific self-study groups would follow. At this initial session, they would meet their chairman and begin formulating their plans for accomplishing the charges made to them.

The Coordinating Committee should resume meeting in September and hold sessions at least another four times throughout the school year. It is conceivable that the final self-evaluation report will be most efficiently put together during meetings of the Coordinating Committee held just after school closes for the pupils. In this way, teachers involved will be able to devote full time to its completion.

TIMETABLE FOR SELF-STUDY GROUPS

The specific self-study groups need to meet frequently throughout the school year. It is wise to arrange for at least four times during the year when pupils are dismissed early and the balance of the day is given over to the staff's work on the self-evaluation. This would include the initial "kick-off" meeting during October followed by other early dismissals in January, March and May. Each one of these sessions should begin with a progress report by the Chairman. His sharing of information of all the group's activities provides a necessary cohesiveness to the project. At some of these sessions, it may be deemed advisable to have a visiting consultant speak to a particular point of inquiry generated by the staff since the self-evaluation began. Perhaps an authority on trends in elementary education would be sought by the self-study groups to get an idea of what new and innovative practices are beginning to take hold.

In addition to the scheduled released time, the specific self-study groups would be meeting after regular pupil dismissal time. Although it would vary with the needs of the group, twice a month would be adequate for most. The exact dates of these sessions should be left to the study group itself. Only the members of each unit know the most advantageous time for meeting. Once established, each group's meeting time would be reported by its leader to the Chairman of the self-evaluation.

Suggested Timetable for Self-Evaluation

May—Superintendent selects Chairman
      Formation of Coordinating Committee
June—First meeting of Coordinating Committee
Summer—Several meetings of Coordinating Committee or a sub-committee to select evaluative
      criteria
September—Second meeting of Coordinating Committee—evaluative criteria adopted, specific
      self-study groups planned
October—Initial "kick-off" total staff meeting*—Self-study group meetings begin
November—Third meeting of Coordinating Committee—Self-study group meetings continue
December—Self-study group meetings continue
January—Second total staff meeting*—progress report—Self-study group meetings continue
February—Fourth meeting of Coordinating Committee—Self-study group meetings continue
March—Third total staff meeting*—Progress report—Self-study group meetings continue
April—Fifth meeting of Coordinating Committee—Self-study group meetings continue
May—Fourth total staff meeting*—Progress report—Self-study group meetings completed;
      final self-study reports sent to Coordinating Committee
June—Sixth meeting of Coordinating Committee—begin assembling of total self-evaluation
      report
Summer—Coordinating Committee or sub-committee complete total self-evaluation report

---

*Early pupil dismissals are suggested for these sessions.

THE FINAL REPORT

As was seen, the final sessions of the Coordinating Committee are devoted to the preparation of the self-evaluation report. This document should be ready for submission to the staff in September of the year following the self-evaluation. At individual faculty meetings, the contents should be reviewed and suggestions received from the teachers. The Coordinating Committee then has the responsibility of taking such suggestions under consideration before the final report is given to the Superintendent. He, in turn, will provide the members of the Board of Education with the document and begin to make plans for its submission to an outside evaluation team.

The contents of the self-evaluation report could include the following:
- The self-evaluation pattern of organization; how it was carried out; its operating schedule
- A listing of the personnel involved in the Coordinating Committee
- The school district's philosophy of education
- A listing of the personnel involved in the specific self-study groups
- Each specific self-study group's report including:
  - Evaluative criteria ratings
  - Additional narrative comments
  - Survey results
  - Pertinent professional articles
  - Building plans, photographs
  - Reports from outside consultants
  - Recommendations for improvement
- General findings, conclusions and recommendations

SUMMARY

We have seen that, while the idea for a district to undergo a self-evaluation could originate from a number of people, it is the superintendent who must seek out a chairman for the self-appraisal project. Responsibilities of this key figure fall into six areas:

1. Over-all leadership of the entire self-evaluation process
2. Selection and inviting cross-section representation to serve on the Coordinating Committee
3. Chairmanship of all sessions of the Coordinating Committee
4. Advice to all work study group sessions
5. Providing the district's administrators with regular progress reports
6. Preparation and submission of periodic reports for the Board of Education

Establishment of the Coordinating Committee requires great care in order to achieve a balanced representation of all schools and categories of positions. Selection may be made from the following:

1. Classroom teachers from various grade levels
2. Principals
3. Special service personnel
4. Subject-matter specialists
5. Board of Education member

6. P.T.A. member
7. Teacher organization member
8. Secondary school teacher
9. Administrative interns
10. Non-professional employees

The work sessions of the Coordinating Committee will find them applying themselves to these responsibilities:

1. Selecting evaluative criteria
2. Establishing a timetable
3. Creating charges for the specific self-study groups
4. Deciding on work areas for all study units
5. Producing regular progress reports for the total staff
6. Preparing material for the local news media
7. Developing the self-evaluation final report

The specific self-study groups formed to investigate areas of the curriculum, physical plant and special services would be comprised of members of the Coordinating Committee, teachers, administrators, and persons whose position is directly related to the area under inquiry. Their functions would include the collection of data, fulfilling the evaluation instrument's requirements, making recommendations and preparing a report for the Coordinating Committee. These groups would gather their data by:

1. Conducting inspection tours
2. Taking inventory
3. Interviewing
4. Surveying
5. Visiting other school systems
6. Engaging visiting consultants

It has been suggested that one year be devoted to the self-evaluation procedure. Summers can be used effectively. During the school year, occasional early dismissals of children and released time for teachers facilitates the progress of the project.

The final report would be expected to include the ratings required by the evaluative instrument, additional comments, survey results, consultants' observations, and recommendations for improvement.

It would be expected that the final report would be reviewed by the staff, administrators and the Board of Education prior to its submission to any visiting evaluation team that has been engaged to review the district's self-assessment.

4

Self-Evaluation
at the Bradley School

A FICTIONAL SCHOOL TAKES ACCOUNT OF ITSELF

There will always be occasions when an individual school initiates the process of self-evaluation because it recognizes the value of the procedure and has a willingness to look in the mirror. The step-by-step activities from the idea of introspection to the implementation of recommendations can be one of the most exciting experiences a school ever has. This chapter devotes itself to a case study of a single school and its entire self-evaluation enterprise. Another school, wishing to follow this account of an evaluation sequence, may vary in procedure in order to suit its own needs. Nevertheless, it is felt that the basic structure of the fictionalized self-study will help any school who undertakes a similar self-improvement project.

AN IDEA IS BORN

Tom Lawrence wanted to be a better-than-ordinary elementary school principal. He had taken the appropriate courses over many years and had adequate formal training for the position. His background included classroom teaching experience and he knew that improving education for the youngsters would always depend upon improving the instruction provided by the teacher. Now, after several years as the chief administrator for Bradley School, Tom felt ready to undertake comprehensive steps to make it one of the best elementary schools in the state. When discussing his feeling about the school's readiness for overall improvement with Dr. Walters, the district superintendent, both men agreed that establishing an objective picture of "what is the present condition of the school" would be a first step. They shared the opinion that a logical initiation for educational advancement at Bradley would be a detailed investigation of the school and its enterprises, comparing the present situation with its stated goals. Recommendations for improvement needed to be made and acted upon in order to have increased achievement of their objectives. Soon Tom Lawrence and Dr. Walters found that they were enthusiastically planning the educational project usually termed "evaluation."

APPROACHING THE ADMINISTRATION

At the next meeting of the district's school administrators, Dr. Walters explained that the Bradley School would seek overall improvement by undertaking a comprehensive self-evaluation process. He pointed out how this may aid the other schools if solutions are found for problems that are common to all. Charles Dempsey, principal of another elementary school asked if evaluation of one school might not unduly focus attention on that building and consequently allow the other's needs to be neglected. Dr. Walters didn't think so. He was optimistic about how the Board of Education could be convinced of the action required to improve the evaluated school and thence easily take the next step to applying the same aid to the others. Also the Superintendent hinted that any success of the self-evaluation process at Bradley could be the signal for the other schools to benefit from their own self-study. Tom Lawrence added the promise that he would make regular reports to the other principals so that they were always knowledgeable about the progress of Bradley's self-investigation.

FACING THE FACULTY

The faculty at Bradley School comprised twenty teachers of grades kindergarten through six. The principal's first mention of the evaluation idea was made to the faculty council that had representation from three units of teachers: Kindergarten through Grade Two, Grades Three and Four, and Grades Five and Six. At Bradley they referred to the divisions as Primary, Middle, and Upper. The group's three members readily saw the value of the Bradley staff being introspective about the school but they were not without questions. Why, asked Sixth Grade Teacher Jennifer Brewster, go through an evaluation in order to get improvements at Bradley? We all know, she said, what our needs are. All we have to do, she maintained, was insist more emphatically that they be met. Mr. Lawrence pointed out the value of the thorough documentation of needs that a self-evaluation made possible and emphasized that a comprehensive justification had a much better chance of persuading administration and the Board of Education than a list gathered on the basis of "I wish we had thus and so."

First Grade Teacher Louise Foster expressed concern that the self-evaluation would damage staff morale by openly revealing individual teacher weaknesses. Principal Lawrence assured her that this was not going to happen. He explained that a total evaluation did not have as its goal an identification of specific negative items about individual personnel. Rather, criteria would be approved in advance by the total faculty and all practices and procedures judged against these. Findings would be expressed relative to situations such as "Arithmetic textbooks are seven years old and omit much of the current thinking of mathematics" and "The use of the overhead projector is limited due to the possession of only two of these units." Mr. Lawrence added that individual evaluation of personnel would not be part of the project and that judgement of staff would continue as always within the confines of mutual confidence between teacher and principal. However, he added, that the method and process of personnel evaluation would be examined.

ORGANIZING FOR SELF-EVALUATION

The Faculty Council presented its unanimous endorsement of the self-evaluation idea to the staff at a general meeting. Again, questions arose and Mr. Lawrence and the three Council members responded. Discussions centered mostly about the criteria to be used as a basis of judgement and the time that would be required to do the job properly. The group approved the formation of a steering committee to investigate both aspects and to report its findings to the faculty for their review. It was felt that the existing Faculty Council comprised of the principal and three representative teacher members was especially suitable to act as the steering committee for the self-evaluation. The Bradley teachers willingly accepted that this made Tom Lawrence the Chairman of the self-study. Although he explained that any staff member could act in that capacity, the group considered him the logical choice.

SEEKING CRITERIA

The Steering Committee lost little time responding to the direction of the faculty. Local colleges, universities, a regional school study council, and the county and state departments of education were contacted to ascertain available evaluative criteria for elementary schools. After several weeks written materials of this nature were forthcoming and the committee began their initial review. They found that different approaches were made by the various authors and that some were not applicable to a single school self-evaluation. Others, however, had categories of investigation that appealed strongly to the committee. Tom Lawrence was especially enthusiastic about one document's criteria for a safe, adaptable school plant. He had hopes of finding better ways of utilizing his building for some instructional innovations. The teachers on the committee were particularly drawn to evaluative criteria that set high standards in the area of instructional aids in the form of materials and equipment for the classroom. The Steering Committee also found that there were some categories, unique to their own goals, that were not adequately covered by any published materials. In this situation they would have to develop their own custom-tailored evaluative standard based on their objectives.

Gathering together the most suitable criteria, the committee carefully checked it with the school district's philosophy of education. Whenever modifications were needed to place the standards in line with the local school's creed, the changes were made.

ESTABLISHING A TIMETABLE

How long, the group wondered, will this introspective exercise take? The Steering Committee realized that one way to decrease the chances for positive outcomes would be to have frequent and long faculty meetings begun with vague direction and ending with obscure accomplishments. Essential were clear concise directions for each participant and frequent progress reports bringing current summations of achievement to the total group.

With this in mind the committee easily agreed on a one year total period of evaluation but there were differences of opinion concerning the number of meetings to be held during that year. Third Grade Teacher Carol Lynch said that she thought there was danger in meeting too seldom because continuity would be lost and enthusiasm would wane. She suggested two or three meetings a week for the specific self-study committees and every other week for the total faculty. Jennifer Brewster didn't agree. She pointed out that the teachers of the upper grades, whom she represented, had most of the extra assignments such as sponsorship of the safety patrol, student council and glee club requiring frequent additional time. She felt that the value of the self-assessment would be lost if teachers turned against it because of its encroachment on their regular responsibilities. Meeting once or twice a month should be sufficient said she.

Teacher Louise Foster and Principal Tom Lawrence were instrumental in helping all to see the hazards of too little or too many meetings. Largely due to their efforts the steering committee arrived at an agreement providing for the following time table.

September—Introduction of idea to faculty council; Faculty council orients total staff; Steering committee organized.
October-May—Specific self-study groups meet once per week on Mondays; steering committee meets the third Wednesday each month; total faculty meets the last Wednesday each month.
June—Steering committee receives all specific self-study group reports.
Summer—Final report prepared.
September—Final report submitted for total faculty consideration
October—Final report submitted to Superintendent.

The steering committee knew that the majority of weekly meetings would have to take place after regular pupil dismissal. However, they received a commitment from the principal that his routine faculty meetings would be limited to those dealing with the most important matters. Information requiring only announcement would be handled via written bulletins issued to those involved. The idea of the final report being written during a few weeks in the summer drew unanimous support from the group. Knowing how vital it is to be able to devote time and energy to any writing project, the committee realized that after-school hours were not conducive to its success. Tom Lawrence secured Dr. Walter's word that he would submit a budget request to the Board of Education for the summer writing of the self-evaluation report.

TEACHER PARTICIPATION

With all of Bradley's teachers going to be involved in the self-study, the steering committee divided the labor of the large undertaking by creating specific self-study committees. They decided on the following units based on the evaluation criteria they had selected:

Physical Plant and Instructional Equipment
Home-School-Community Relations

Library Services
Language Arts
Mathematics and Science
Social Studies
Health and Physical Education
The Arts

Each sub-group had at least one teacher from grades kindergarten through three and another from grades four through six. Although the decision could be made differently elsewhere the Bradley steering committee allowed for three teachers to be on the specific self-study committees investigating Physical Plant and Instructional Equipment, Home-School-Community Relations, Language Arts, and Mathematics and Science. In addition to the teacher representation, specialists in art and music were invited to the Arts group, the librarian to the Library Services section, the reading specialist to the Language Arts unit, and the physical education specialist and the nurse to the Health and Physical Education committee. It was expected that A-V specialists, maintenance and custodial personnel, and representative parents would be called in by the various groups as they investigated areas involving their interests.

Principal Tom Lawrence and Superintendent Dr. Walters were asked to visit each group from time to time in order to provide consultative assistance. Also they expressed a willingness to seek the aid of authorities specializing in a particular field. These individuals could be engaged to consult with a group seeking elaboration of some aspect of their investigation. The local school study council, neighborhood districts, and colleges and universities could be the source of such people.

SELF-STUDY ACTIVITIES

During the first Monday in October the specific self-study groups began their meetings. With each group comprising three or four staff members it was perfectly suitable to have each of the eight groups meet in various classrooms. The Library Services group was typical of these study units. Joanne Burton, representing the primary grades, and Jennifer Brewster, the upper grades, were joined by librarian Karen Carlson and the district's Audio-Visual Coordinator, Harold Bates. Their first order of business was to select their own chairman. There was some discussion about the possibility of bias in the direction of pro-book or pro-A-V if the librarian or A-V coordinator were selected to lead the group. Then the group unanimously selected sixth grade teacher Jennifer Brewster as their chairman. She immediately appointed first grade teacher Louise Foster as the group's recorder to take notes and prepare progress reports for the steering committee.

Copies of the school's philosophy and the evaluative criteria were made available to each committee member. Chairman Brewster asked all to familiarize themselves with these materials and to give thought to how best their research should be done in order to effectively judge themselves against the standards. It was at their second meeting that this took the form of a list of plausible activities for the self-study group. Karen Carlson, the librarian, agreed to gather information concerning standards of good libraries issued by the American Library Association. She also volunteered to make arrangements to have the group visit a school library nearby that she knew was considered to be one of the best in the area. A-V coordinator Harold Bates wanted to share material he had on hand from the Department of Audio-Visual Instruction of the National Education Association. He said the literature was now describing how the library and audio-visual aids departments were being coupled into multi-media centers for learning. He had recently taken a course at the local state college that covered the latest trends in this development. The group enthusiastically endorsed his idea of inviting the professor to visit with them to share his ideas.

Mrs. Brewster realized the need to take careful inventory of everything the Bradley School Library had in its collection and to have a description of the services that it offered. It was decided that the best meeting place for the group each Monday was not in a classroom but rather in the library itself so that this accounting could be done by all.

Teacher Joanne Burton submitted that it was important to ascertain faculty members' opinions concerning their use of the library. After some discussion of the contribution each teacher might make the Chairman asked that Miss Burton draw up a brief questionnaire that could be sent to each teacher. The self-study group would review it and submit it to each of the faculty.

Subsequent meetings of the Library Services self-study group saw the completion of the survey form to be given to the teachers. It read as follows:

Date

Dear _____   _____
          Teacher's Name

     The Library Services self-study group would not want its investigation to exclude your views in this area. Please take a moment to give us your ideas in response to the following general questions. Return this survey sheet to the undersigned, Room 20, by November 20.

I. Please comment relative to the following aspects of improved library services:
    A. Developing our present facility into a multi-media resource center.

    B. Areas where our present collection needs additional books and materials.

    C. Suggested changes in the arrangement of our total collection.

    D. Suggested changes in the system of withdrawing books and materials from the library.

    E. Suggested changes in the way in which the facility is available to teachers and their classes.

    F. Ways in which services and facilities can be improved to better serve independent study by individual students.

II. Any other comment:

Many thanks,

Jennifer Brewster, Chairman
Library Services Self-Study
Committee, Bradley School

As a follow-up to the collection of the survey, it was decided that one or two teachers who were particularly responsive to the questionnaire should be interviewed. Realizing the limitations of the survey method, Joanne Burton volunteered to speak with the most interested teachers in order to gain greater elaboration of their opinions concerning library improvement.

Karen Carlson was successful in arranging for the group to visit another school district's library. One of the Monday afternoons would be used to go to the new Scottsfield School in nearby Jordantown. However, the non-librarians in the group had reservations about their ability to observe the facility intelligently and to ask the librarian key questions in order to return fortified with information that would be valuable to their self-study. Consequently, they decided on a guide for themselves before the visit. It read as follows:

LIBRARY SERVICES SELF-STUDY COMMITTEE

Bradley School

Guide For Library Visitation

I.   Materials
    A. What is available?
    B. How are they selected? By whom?
    C. How are they cataloged?
    D. How are they displayed?

II. Equipment, Facilities and Personnel
   A. What is the physical organization?
   B. What equipment is utilized?
   C. What audio-visual aids are available?
   D. What personnel are employed? Their responsibilities?
III. Procedures
   A. How do classes use the facility?
   B. What provision is made for independent study by individual students?
   C. How are materials produced? What are they?
   D. How can teachers use the services?

Miss Burton, Mrs. Brewster, and Mr. Bates each took responsibility for a section of their visitation guide. Librarian Karen Carlson was left free to ask all those questions that could not be anticipated in advance. As a librarian, she would be skilled enough to develop inquiries as she viewed the neighboring library first-hand.

ADDITIONAL SELF-STUDY METHODS

During these activities of the Library Services self-study group the other units were also busily engaged in data gathering. The Physical Plant and Instructional Equipment group not only toured their own school facility but also visited several nearby schools of similar size, one very like their own in design and the other very different in both appearance and program. Tom Lawrence and Superintendent Walters both had enough interest to accompany the group on their field trips.

The Home-School-Community Relations unit invited one of the town's Councilmen to visit with them and describe community recreational, library and safety needs. It was revealing to learn how much of this related directly to the school's offerings to its pupils. This group also invited a representative parents' group to offer reaction to reporting procedures including both written type and conferencing. The parents were impressed with the Bradley teachers willingness to listen and their desire to improve their procedures. As he visited with this group, Principal Tom Lawrence reflected how this activity had the wonderful by-product of good public relations.

The academic self-study groups concerned with Language Arts, Mathematics and Science, Social Studies, Health and Physical Education, and the Arts were collecting information about themselves by examining their goals, courses of study, and books and materials. They made comparisons of these with the evaluative criteria and sought outside assistance to hear of other schools' activities in the subject area they had under study. The local school study council was helpful by arranging for some of the principals and subject matter specialists from outside districts to stop by to speak to the groups about the latest trends in their area of expertise.

THE PRINCIPAL'S ROLE

Realizing that he was mainly responsible for the entire evaluation enterprise at Bradley, Principal Tom Lawrence kept "on top" of the situation throughout the meetings of the sub-groups. He visited their Monday conferences and made helpful suggestions in an effort to facilitate the work of the committees with other schools, professors at local colleges, and the school study council. Not to be dismissed lightly was the encouragement and the ideas he gave to the study groups when they faced an obstacle to their progress. Mr. Lawrence spoke with the various chairmen throughout the week to ascertain how things were going and what, if any, assistance was required.

When the recorders from each self-study unit submitted their reports from their Monday meetings, Mr. Lawrence studied what was happening and shared this with his steering committee at their monthly gathering. Here they decided where additional help might be required, what materials needed to be secured, or who would be the best resource person for a group seeking this aid. This representative coordinating group prepared a report for presentation each month to the total faculty. This proved to be an important procedure because teachers then had knowledge of each group's progress and common problems could be discussed.

SHARING IDEAS

It was during one of the meetings of the steering committee that it was decided to bring in one of the authors of the evaluative criteria that Bradley had selected as the basis for its self-study. This gentleman, Dr. Lorton Calvin, now held a position in the State Department of Education and welcomed the opportunity to speak to the Bradley faculty. Dr. Calvin revealed the history concerned with the development of the criteria and told of some of the difficult decisions the authors had in arriving at standards of excellence in some of the areas. He was asked by Mrs. Lynch if it was appropriate to "up-grade" the standards of some of the criteria when the Bradley staff had ambitions exceeding those in the evaluation instrument. It was just the kind of question Dr. Calvin wanted. "By all means," he said, "I support every bit of your desire to take that extra stride. Your educational program should be what this community requires and no criteria committed to paper—even when I was the author—should place a ceiling on your goals."

As he had promised, Tom Lawrence prepared regular oral reports for his fellow-administrators. Dr. Walters called on him frequently to tell the status of Bradley's self-evaluation. Questions from the other principals were in quantity. What was the reaction of the staff? Were parents inquiring about the evaluation? Where did he find the time for such a project? Who were the consultants? What did they say? Where were visitations made? What did they see? Mr. Lawrence welcomed the inquiries because he was satisfied that Bradley's introspection was going well. Dr. Walters was also delighted at the interest shown because he felt it would mean that some of the other school leaders would follow Bradley's pioneering efforts.

INFORMING THE BOARD

The Board of Education was kept abreast of the Bradley School's self-process by Dr. Walters. At mid-year he had Tom Lawrence come in to a public Board meeting to tell of the procedure and progress to that point. Mr. Lawrence became well-versed in these presentations by keeping his Parent-Teacher Organization informed and by speaking to school administrators affiliated with the school study council. John Thatcher, the Board of Education President, was interested enough to ask if he could sit in on one of the self-study group sessions to get first-hand knowledge of its procedures. This was accomplished and thereafter Mr. Thatcher was a staunch advocate of self-assessment on a local level. His previous doubts concerning approval of some of the budget items related to the evaluation all but disappeared.

PREPARING THE FINAL REPORT

The reports from each of the eight specific self-study groups began to reach the Steering Committee in May. By the end of the school year in June all were submitted. Included in each were the participant's names and responsibilities, the evaluative criteria ratings, often with additional narrative comments, results of surveys, questionnaires and interviews, reports from outside consultants and descriptions of places visited. Some of the reports also included pertinent professional articles, photographs of visited facilities, and summations of readings done by committee members. Recommendations for improvement in the studied area highlighted each of the group reports.

SUMMER PLANNING

As chairman of the Steering Committee, Tom Lawrence worked with Dr. Walters to plan a session during the summer when his group could prepare the self-evaluation final report. It was agreed that three weeks in July would be used for this purpose and that the three teacher representatives of the primary, middle, and upper grades of the school would be paid for their participation. A secretary was also assigned to prepare the copy for its presentation to the Bradley staff in September.

Immediately past the Fourth of July holiday, the steering committee comprising First Grade Teacher Louise Foster, Third Grade Teacher Carol Lynch, Sixth Grade Teacher Jennifer Brewster, and Principal Tom Lawrence gathered at the now empty Bradley School and met each day free of their usual responsibilities. Their task was to review the reports from the eight self-study groups and to compile this information into a final report with recommendations.

Chairman Lawrence assumed the responsibilities of a preface to the report that related a brief history of the school and a description of how the self-evaluation was organized and carried out. For the benefit of other schools interested in the process, he included the time table followed and the responsibilities of each working group.

Miss Foster's suggestion that each faculty member be listed with a brief outline of their educational training and experience was accepted. Also each teacher's role in the evaluation enterprise was included. Mrs. Brewster's idea of having the elementary school's philosophy of education precede the self-study analysis was unanimously agreed to.

FINAL REPORT FORMAT

The steering committee proof-read each sub group's report carefully and made corrections whenever necessary. There were some statements requiring rephrasing of content in order to keep similar the general style of reporting. Particular attention was paid to each group's recommendations. Mrs. Lynch put forward the idea of repeating all of the recommendations in the final pages of the report so that the faculty, the Superintendent and the Board of Education would have a comprehensive picture of the desired improvements to Bradley School as seen through the eyes of its staff. After some discussion it was decided to go along with this suggestion and to have the report in a loose-leaf format so that any section, especially the list of recommendations, could be separated when particular study was to be made of those pages.

Typing of the final report began soon after the steering committee ended its three week preparation of the materials. The secretary wisely placed its contents on spirit duplicating masters so that the copy could be easily made in quantity for the Bradley staff's review. Also, minor corrections were able to be made by Tom Lawrence by directly writing on the master without requiring re-typing of an entire page.

THE FACULTY REVIEWS THEIR WORK

When school re-opened in September, the principal allowed a few weeks for the important task of getting school started. Then he called a faculty meeting just for the purpose of distributing and having preliminary discussion on the self-evaluation final report. He and members of the steering committee described the reasons for its format and answered some initial questions from the teachers. All were asked to spend a week reading the document and to make notes on any additions, omissions, or questions that came to mind.

During the second meeting of the faculty the following points were made:

Standardized test results ought to be included so that the measured intelligence and level of achievement of Bradley students would be available as background information.

More biographical detail should be given about each of the consultants who visited with the self-study groups.

Present class sizes and the results of a recent projected enrollment study should be inserted in the report.

It should be pointed out that some of the recommendations have already been carried out. No reason was seen to delay those that had acceptance of all and required no additional funding.

Appropriate modifications concerning these suggestions were made to the final document whenever the majority agreed to them. Typing of the corrected copy was completed and the report was submitted to the Superintendent, Dr. Walters. He, in turn, made copies available to each Board of Education member and scheduled review of its contents on the Board's agenda for future meetings. Dr. Walters liked Tom Lawrence's suggestion that he and his steering committee would be pleased to discuss any aspect of the document with the Board. He added that he may also request Mr. Lawrence to do likewise with the administrative group.

ACTING UPON RECOMMENDATIONS

As the Bradley faculty continued to meet during the school year they confronted themselves with their own recommendations that had come forth from their self-evaluation. Some could be enacted with little, if any, additional funds and were largely within the power of the faculty itself. Discussions on how to best implement the following kinds of recommendations were held:

> The kinds of independent seatwork given to children when the teacher is working with a small segment of the class should include creative writing, recreational reading, use of a listening station or viewing filmstrips. Narrow workbook completion activities should be kept to a minimum.

> More pupil interaction should be emphasized in reading discussions. Role-playing, dialogue, and choral speaking should be practiced more frequently, replacing concentration on a question and answer.

> Grouping within a class should be encouraged in spelling. Challenging word lists should be culled from the children's lessons in the other subjects. Each child should have additional spelling words that require his individual attention for their mastery.

BOARD OF EDUCATION INVOLVEMENT

Dr. Walters, as superintendent, conferred with Tom Lawrence about those recommendations that required Board of Education approval. The two men decided that it was not wise to wait until budget request time to mention the recommendations necessitating additional funds. Instead, a general discussion of the thinking behind the Bradley faculty's suggestions would first be led by Dr. Walters and Mr. Lawrence with the Board of Education. The types of recommendations treated in this way were as follows:

> In-service educational workshops should be held for teachers in Physical Education. There is a need for the general classroom teacher to learn activities, skills, and techniques in Physical Education, an area requiring increased emphasis in the education of our children.

> A search should be made for a standardized testing program that would adequately evaluate the present mathematics curriculum at Bradley. It is obvious that the traditional mathematics tests do not properly cope with the arithmetical offerings in our school.

> It is urged that the valuable practice of parent-teacher conferences be given more time by dismissing pupils early on four days. This should be in lieu of one written report and include every parent.

> An effort should be made to relocate the special education class. Present housing of this small group is inadequate in terms of space and facilities. Perhaps a portable classroom could be rented until suitable permanent quarters could be arranged.

> Consideration should be given to engaging an outside evaluation team comprised of specialists in the categories studied in the self-evaluation. This visiting group could objectively analyze the needs of the school based on their own observation and thorough study of the self-evaluation findings.

REACTION TO SELF-INQUIRY

Of course, the recommendations being considered by the Board of Education and those contemplated by the Bradley faculty were not all endorsed and acted upon immediately. However, both groups were now very much aware of ways in which increasingly effective education could take place at that school. The teachers, particularly, were more thoroughly knowledgeable of their total school's strengths and weaknesses than most staffs. Their efforts to improve became a team effort and as Third Grade Teacher Carol Lynch said, "After this self-evaluation no one knows us as well as we know ourselves. We're proud of our past accomplishments and, even more important, we are clear on the specific steps we need to take in order to do even better in the years to come."

5

The Visiting Team:
Its Composition and Organization

Second only in importance to the self-evaluation process is the identification, selection, recruitment and orientation of a visiting team. The school district will do well to settle for nothing short of the very best in the way of team membership. The composition of the team should include outstanding specialists who possess a comprehensive understanding of modern elementary educational practices. Participants should be chosen for their proven performance, mature professional judgment and general staff acceptance as master teachers and educational leaders.

For the present, in most states, the evaluation of elementary schools is not a function of an established state or regional accrediting group. Statewide efforts toward evaluation largely emanate from the various state departments of education. These departments usually accredit elementary schools with some legal compulsion behind their programs such as determining the school district's eligibility for state aid or establishing the district's entitlement to state disbursement of federal funds. By and large, such evaluations are not very comprehensive. They frequently omit or treat superficially any attempt at self-evaluation, seeking primarily to determine statutory compliance on the part of the school district.

It is indeed encouraging to note that since 1960 better than half the state departments of education have initiated some form of new action or investigation into the field of public elementary school accreditation. Most of these research efforts have been directed toward more significant in-depth studies of schools with the improvement of instruction as the principle objective. Despite all this activity, movement in the direction of finding improved evaluation techniques and procedures has not yet developed to the point where local administrators can universally look to their state departments for both creative leadership and practical assistance in conducting evaluations of quality and substance.

SELF-GENERATED PROGRAMS

Impatient with the steady but slow pace of statewide developments in the area of elementary evaluation, an ever growing number of schools have initiated voluntary, self-generated assessment programs. These schools have had to establish their own criteria for the selection and training of visiting team personnel. State departments of education will be well served by taking a hard look at what these trail-blazing districts have accomplished. These independent evaluations are large motivated by a genuine desire to probe for specific strength or weakness with a view toward effecting constructive change. Evaluations of this type are almost certain to be more comprehensive than are those conducted by state departments of education operating solely under legal compulsions. Some school districts limit elementary evaluation efforts to the self-evaluation process explained in Chapter 4; however, most go on to include an outside visiting team. Districts which take this step, generally agree that the increased benefits which accrue to the schools and the community more than justify the effort, time and expense involved in utilizing the services of visiting experts.

COMPOSITION OF THE VISITING TEAM

The composition of the visiting evaluation team should be directly related to the purposes to be served. Teams will, and certainly should, vary in size and specialties represented in accordance with the demands for either a full or partial investigation of one, several or many elementary schools. The evaluative criteria selected by the staff for its self-analysis will also have a very definite bearing upon the makeup and size of the visiting team. For example, if the criteria chosen afford ample opportunities to self-evaluate the adequacy of buildings and grounds, then it would be quite essential that one or more visiting specialists in that field be included within the team membership. Likewise, if the criteria employed provide for extensive review of all available special education services and programs, then surely an expert in special education ought to be recruited to serve as a vital resource person and a principal respondent to that section of the self-evaluation instrument. A team comprised of specialists selected in response to the areas treated by the self-evaluative criteria offers by far the greater promise for productive outcomes.

A visitation team of five or six members is considered to be the smallest workable number capable of producing adequate and acceptable results. Teams that are too small cannot cover fully all of the areas undergoing evaluation. Their work will of necessity offer only spotty coverage and therefore will be decidedly less effective in fostering needed improvements. A committee which exceeds fifteen members functions too slowly and consumes an inordinate amount of its limited visitation time in the resolution of internal management matters. The ideal team size is to be found somewhere between these two extremes. Schools which use self-evaluative criteria calling for extensive coverage of many aspects of the elementary school program will undoubtedly require the services of teams which more closely approximate the maximum recommended size.

Teams are very frequently formed to include, in addition to an all important chairman, specialists in each of the major areas as follows:
1. elementary administration
2. kindergarten-primary

3. middle or intermediate grade education
4. upper grade education (in K-8 organizations)
5. subject matter specialists
6. special educational services
7. school buildings, grounds and facilities
8. educational technology and instructional materials

Where appropriate to the purposes to be served, experts in non-graded organization, the middle school, programmed instruction, elementary libraries, and the like, may be added to the team either as regular members or as special consultants.

IDENTIFICATION AND SELECTION OF TEAM MEMBERS

The recruitment of an outstanding visiting team of elementary specialists will present many challenging opportunities for both school administrators and the self-evaluation team. Every effort should be directed toward identifying and convincing top talent to serve. Individuals chosen must have, or be able to secure and retain, the respect, confidence and good will of teachers and administrators. Also, they must relate well to community leaders, board of education members, P.T.A. groups, professional and non-professional support personnel and a host of other individuals or groups who stand at the center or periphery of evaluation involvement.

Once the self-evaluative criteria has been selected and the number and specialties to be represented on the team established, the entire faculty should be invited to suggest likely candidates for team membership. Lists of nominees for each specialty must then be compiled and the chief school officer, acting jointly with the chairman of the self-evaluation committee, should now begin the process of determining which persons are to receive priority consideration. It will be well at this point to seek the guidance and assistance of both the administrative council and the self-evaluation committee in arriving at these important decisions. Discreet outside inquiries should be undertaken in all cases where primary sources of information regarding team candidates are limited.

In the evaluation team recruitment sequence, several options are open for local consideration. A number of schools have chosen to concentrate first upon the selection of a person to fill the very important post of team chairman. These schools have seen such a procedure as being much preferred since it affords opportunities for a chairman, so selected, to offer comment regarding standards and prerequisites for team participation. Districts employing this practice report greater success with team recruitment since potential members more readily accept team assignment when they know exactly under whose direction they will be working. It is further argued that, early selection allows for the chairman's full orientation to school and community thus strengthening his leadership role with the team.

Some schools, after careful forethought, have avoided early designation of a chairman for fear that he might influence too greatly the entire team selection process. A further concern raised is the likelihood that a chairman's objectivity could be substantially diminished if he were to engage in frequent pre-evaluation discussion and decision making sessions with the school administration and the self-evaluation committee. All facts in the matter weighed, it must be concluded that the advantages of early chairman selection by far outweigh the case for delay. If a chairman of the highest caliber is selected, a person of vast professional experience and training, one who also enjoys an unquestioned reputation in the field of interpersonal relationships, then certainly the early participation of such an individual in the evaluation effort should be encouraged rather than feared.

LIKELY SOURCES OF CHAIRMEN AND TEAM MEMBERS

Chairmen for elementary school evaluation teams are often located from within the ranks of: college presidents, deans of schools of education, county superintendents of schools and district superintendents of schools. Team members are frequently recruited from among professors of early childhood and elementary education, curriculum coordinators and assistant superintendents for instruction, elementary principals, buildings and grounds specialists, subject area supervisors, child study team personnel and career teachers. Of course, no listing of this type can be all inclusive. There are many other position titles and categories which should not be overlooked. As was pointed out earlier in this chapter, the entire faculty should be encouraged to suggest names of persons who have demonstrated personal and professional potential for this important service. Presidents of learned societies and educational associations at national, regional and state levels should be contacted for names of suitable candidates. Other school systems which have recently assembled visiting teams may likewise prove to be most helpful sources of information.

ORIENTATION OF THE TEAM

A visiting team cannot be expected to work productively without adequate orientation. Once team selections have been made and acceptances received, plans should progress for the orientation of team members. Not only will they require orientation to the school and community, but they will also need direction concerning roles and functions within the team structure.

Throughout the many months of work by the self-evaluation committee, materials will have been gathered or developed which will prove of value to the visiting team's understanding of the local scene. For example, most self-evaluation criteria, and therefore final evaluation reports, include one or more sections devoted to the historical background and sociological evolution of the community. It is important for team members to know something of the history, growth rate, ethnic origins and occupational composition of the community whose schools they have been invited to assess. If material of this nature is not treated in the self-evaluation committee's report, it will need to be developed for team orientation use. Facts about the local tax structure, type and age of home dwellings, immigration and out-migration rates of school age children, industrial and residential zoning, and a host of other pertinent data affecting a deeper understanding of the schools and community should be woven into the self-evaluation report or included in a brief companion document. Later in the chapter, additional recommendations will be made with regard to specific background materials for team distribution.

Most visitation teams experience difficulty in meeting for even the briefest periods of time prior to the actual evaluation. This is especially true of teams drawn from a wide geographical radius. It is quite to be expected that members will not be together long enough before the visitation for much in-person orientation to occur. Prepared statements, reports, briefing papers and summaries, will, of necessity and for the most part, form the backbone of the school-community orientation effort.

The visiting team's schedule is usually arranged so that the team arrives in the community during the late afternoon or early evening of the day preceding the evaluation. During these few hours before evaluation starts, many internal decisions must be made for the deployment and utilization of personnel. Committee and sub-committee assignments, as well as individual tasks and responsibilities, must form the principal order of business. The school administration and self-evaluation committee should not expect that the team could possibly manage an extensive school-community orientation session as an addition to its already imposing organizational agenda. Therefore, much of the team's initial understanding of the school and community will have to be garnered from prepared materials submitted in advance of the visit.

School administrators and self-evaluation committee members will want to be present to welcome the visiting team as it arrives for the pre-evaluation planning session. At this time, if the team requires clarification or amplification of the background materials already furnished, this should be offered with due consideration of the team's restricted time schedule and the heavy workload for the evening.

TEAM ORGANIZATION

If the chairman of the visiting team is selected some months prior to the evaluation visit he will be able to devote considerable thought and planning to the organization of the team for productive appraisal. The nature of the self-evaluation criteria, size of the team, length of the visitation, number of specialties represented on the team, as well as the size and number of schools to be evaluated, will all have a very direct influence upon the emergence of a team's organizational pattern. Generally speaking, teams function best when the respective specialists do not work in total isolation, concentrating only upon one area of expertise. Committee members are most effective when they assume the role of chief resource persons in their major fields while at the same time rendering a much wider range of services and assistance to the group as a whole. The Chairman should avoid, at all costs, his involvement in committee or sub-committee assignments. He must be free to devote full time and attention to the weighty responsibilities of coordinating the work of the team. The many alternatives and possibilities for team organization will be detailed in Chapter 6, *The Visiting Team at Work.*

THE VISITING TEAM'S RELATIONSHIP TO THE NUMBER AND SIZE OF SCHOOLS

A visiting team of from five to fifteen members can normally provide for a thorough evaluation of one to six elementary schools, in a single school district, within a two or three day span of time. This projection assumes that the school enrollment averages no more than 600 students per building. Larger school districts or districts with heavier enrollments per building must provide for a longer period of evaluation time proportional to their size or consider the appointment of several teams. The latter recommendation is much preferred since the impact of the evaluation, as well as its reliability and validity, will be lessened considerably by the long process involved in a single team's assessment of a large number of elementary units. Also, visiting team members will undoubtedly have limited time to commit to the district. If the visitation team invitation requires that more than three days be spent away from regular duties, many of the most qualified and able potential team members will decline to serve. Further, it can be stated with certainty that the very involved and demanding 'round the clock nature of visiting team work, in and of itself, precludes a longer period of service. In all instances where the number and size of schools require the use of multi-teams, the uniformity of assessment performance can be greatly enhanced by added attention to the details of team selection and orientation.

BACKGROUND MATERIALS VITAL TO THE TEAM'S FUNCTION

The work of the visiting team is greatly facilitated if the evaluation planners make careful provisions for furnishing each member with all the pertinent materials essential to a productive review and appraisal. The decisions as to what is or is not essential to the smooth and effective operation of the visiting team should not be left to one person alone. It is recommended that a sub-committee of the self-evaluation group be appointed to draw up an all inclusive listing of items which should be forwarded to members of the visiting team. Great care must be exercised to insure that the team is not overburdened with materials having little or no relationship to its performance role. With this consideration in mind, it would be well to have the entire self-evaluation committee review the sub-committee's list to be doubly certain that only essential items are included and that nothing of importance has been overlooked. A representative sample of items to be furnished team members is presented later in this chapter.

TIMING THE DISTRIBUTION TO TEAM MEMBERS

Having established that "what" background materials go to the team is indeed critical to the success of its work, there must also be given much thought to "when" to forward the agreed upon items. A reasonably sound generalization to make is that, by and large, the bulk of background information provided team members is best digested and utilized if it is forwarded well in advance of the team's evaluation target date. Bear in mind that the team members, assuming they have been selected with discrimination, will be among the most busy and productive persons in their respective fields. Materials sent to them too far in advance will stand a strong chance of going unread and being mislaid. The most appropriate time to begin materials distribution is approximately thirty days prior to the date set for the team's visit to the community. It is at this point in time that the personal interest of the evaluators heightens and they become most receptive to any and all attempts to prepare them to render the utmost service to the impending assessment.

It should be noted that some few materials may be withheld for distribution and discussion upon the team's arrival. There may also be justification for delaying the issuance of one or more items until a timely moment during the course of the team's evaluation visit. Cautious consideration should be the byword when dealing with the delayed introduction of facts to be digested by the team as they engage actively in the many demanding tasks of the actual visitation. It is understandable that some background materials may be withheld until the team arrives simply because the local board of education did not act upon them in time to permit inclusion in earlier mailings. Progress reports on innovative pilot projects in such areas as staffing, curriculum, teaching methods, and the like, may intentionally or unintentionally be timed to coincide with the outside visitation team's arrival. If managed with care, the presentation of particulars surrounding such activities can stimulate and further motivate team efforts. Be assured, however, that the widespread, last minute introduction of new or vastly altered information concerning the schools is certain to produce an adverse effect serving only to demoralize and confound the visiting team. Such a situation must be avoided at all costs.

THE STANDARD BACKGROUND MATERIALS PACKET

The Self-Evaluation Report is, of course, the principle document to be included in any background materials packet prepared for the visiting team. This should be a complete copy of the final text as accepted by the self-evaluation committee, faculty, administration and board of education. Without the self-evaluation report the team cannot be expected to function. The chief duty of the visiting team is to offer expert response to the Self-Evaluation Report. If there is one item which must be placed in the hands of each member a full thirty days before the planned visit, it is the Self-Evaluation Report.

Experience has shown that there are a number of standard items in addition to the Self-Evaluation Report which the team will appreciate receiving prior to the start of their work. These materials include:

1. Individual teacher daily or weekly class schedules showing grade level, time allotment for subjects and room numbers.
2. Detailed building floor plans which identify classroom, special purpose rooms, gymnasiums, auditoriums, cafeterias, etc. It is helpful if each classroom shown is further identified as to teacher assigned, grade level and room number.
3. Schedules showing utilization or assignment of special areas such as: library, gymnasium, auditorium, cafeteria, playground, etc.

4. List of assemblies, special programs and featured events which are scheduled to occur during the visitation period.
5. Faculty directories which include teacher names, subject or grade level assignments, as well as, any extra duty responsibilities or co-curricular activities.
6. Guide to the location of all supporting reference and resource materials which have been set aside for use by the visiting team.
7. Roster of self-evaluation committee and sub-committee assignments.

SUMMARY

A visiting team comprised of carefully recruited "outside" elementary education experts can make significant contributions to the work already accomplished by a local self-evaluation committee. Most schools undergoing evaluation elect to engage such a team because of the many benefits its services afford the district.

Matters related to the identification, selection and orientation of visiting team members deserve the utmost attention of the school administration and the self-evaluation committee. Visiting teams will vary in size and composition in direct relationship to the purposes to be served. Generally speaking, teams should include a minimum of five members if reasonably complete review is to be expected. Teams which exceed fifteen persons are too large to be fully responsive in a two or three day evaluation visit situation. The whole staff should participate in suggesting names of likely team members. Professional groups, as well as nearby schools which have completed evaluations, should be contacted for additional information concerning team nominees. The chief school officer and the self-evaluation committee chairman must rank team candidates. First choices and alternates for the chairmanship and the various specialties to be represented should then be presented to the administrative council and the self-evaluation committee for final review and assent. The chairman of the team should be chosen early in the process and his leadership position reinforced by a full and complete orientation to the school and community.

The detailed orientation of team members must largely be carried on through written background materials distributed well in advance of the visit. This approach is resorted to, of necessity, since teams usually find it inconvenient to meet before the evaluation due to heavy personal schedules or travel distances involved. Upon arrival, teams should not be subjected to protracted and extensive orientation to school and community. In-person orientation should be restricted to clarification and the briefest form of elaboration of the prepared background materials already sent to the members. New or revised information, presented at the last moment, can handicap the team's work schedule. The main task of the team at its first session, on the eve of evaluation, is to organize and self-structure so that the most productive outcomes might be forthcoming. It is recommended that the Chairman remain free of committee assignments so that he can coordinate the many aspects of the total review.

Whatever agreements are made regarding the assorted contents of a background materials packet for the team, it should be clearly understood that a copy of the self-evaluation final report is an essential. This document is the basis for team appraisal and response and it should be made available to the team at least thirty days prior to the visitation.

6

The Visiting Team at Work

The elementary schools of our nation rarely have the benefit of being appraised by a group of educators not employed by their own district. The experience of following the process of self-evaluation with an impartial analysis by an outside team of knowledgeable schoolmen is far superior to any review elementary schools can make of themselves. This chapter will relate the mechanics of how these visitors will proceed from their arrival in the to-be-evaluated district until their departure. The host schools have preparations to make for accommodating the visiting team during their work sessions, their school observations, and their overnight stay. The district has decisions to make concerning the personnel they will assign to aid the visitors, the places they will allocate for meetings and the arrangements for presentation of community leaders to the evaluators.

It is advisable to gather both visitors and staff before any of the formal process of evaluation takes place. This is accomplished well by a dinner meeting held prior to the first day of observation. Also the team requires time to hear its chairman outline the methodology and agenda of the next several days to be spent visiting the schools. Hour by hour scheduling is vital to the efficient performance of the team. Each member must know his specific task and provisions must be made for combining individual observations into a comprehensive report.

All this must be accomplished while the schools are functioning in their usual fashion. Viewing a situation that is not a normal day-to-day operation defeats the objectivity required for true evaluation. Class procedures remain the same and student activities are not in any way modified. After pupil dismissal, however, arrangements for evaluators to engage staff members in conversation are most desirable.

The preparation of the visiting team's evaluation report begins during their stay at the district to be assessed. A preliminary presentation is made to the staff just prior to the outsiders' departure. Frequently a post-evaluation meeting is held by the evaluators at a later date. After compilation of the group's complete report their chairman may return to the district to detail his team's account for the Board of Education and school administration.

PREPARATORY ACTIVITIES

Prior to the actual evaluation time it is essential that a meeting of the district superintendent and the self-evaluation chairman be held with the chairman of the visiting team. This gathering can result in decisions concerning the dates of the visitors' arrival, their observation schedule, reporting procedures, and overnight accommodations. Any requests of the chairman concerning materials required, work areas, scheduling, and personnel he wishes his team to meet can be discussed. These topics are best resolved a month or more before the visitation so that adequate time is given for their preparation. In addition, it is desirable to have the team chairman visit the district several weeks before the group arrives. He can become familiar first-hand with the physical arrangements and confirm the planned procedures with the district's educational leaders.

The October or November following the school year of self-evaluation is the best time for the outside team to visit the school system. As discussed in Chapter 5, two or three days are required for an adequate evaluation of a district comprising less than six schools. The materials for the visitors must be ready to be placed in their hands upon their arrival or, with some items, be forwarded by mail prior to their visit. This is especially true of the most important document of all, the self-evaluation report. This should be sent to each evaluator for his review at least thirty days before he arrives in the district to be assessed.

MEETING AREAS

The chairman of the schools' self-evaluation is the key figure in making arrangements at the local level for the outside evaluators' visit. He must concern himself with providing work space for the visitors that is adequate for their number and private enough to permit their uninterrupted conferencing. Possibly appropriate may be the place where the Board of Education meets, one of the school's libraries, or any room that can be adapted for conferencing with large tables, comfortable chairs, adequate ventilation and nearby lavatory facilities. Further, it is advisable that each school to be visited have an area designated as most appropriate for the evaluators to gather as they require. This may vary from school to school. Some have conference rooms ideally suited to this purpose, others can offer their teachers' rooms and, in some cases, unused classrooms can be furnished for their meetings.

PRINCIPAL'S AVAILABILITY

The obvious choice to be host for each of the elementary schools is the principal. He should be advised to clear his calendar of any commitment that would have him out of the building during the evaluation period. Also, appointments that need not take place for those few days should be scheduled for another time permitting the principal to be available for consultation with any member of the visiting team. A hospitable idea is to have a few mothers of the PTA prepare simple refreshments for the evaluators that can be enjoyed both before and after their observations. Most schools have easy-to-follow floor plans to aid visitors in their buildings. These will be welcome by the touring evaluators. When the physical plant is especially complex a principal may assign pupil guides to provide assistance to the assessors as they seek to locate the areas they are observing.

ACCOMMODATIONS FOR THE EVALUATORS

Overnight accommodations for the visiting evaluators should be reserved before their arrival. Ideal for this purpose is a local motel offering rooms comfortable for one or two persons. Frequently these establishments have restaurants on their premises that can provide breakfast and dinner for the evaluation group. (Lunches can be arranged for the visitors in those schools with cafeterias or in a nearby eating place.)

Some motels have small conference areas that are ideal for working sessions of the team during the after dinner hours. The advantages of this accommodation are the uninterrupted privacy of the group and the avoidance of traveling to a school meeting place each evening. Occasionally a motel provides the additional service of transporting a small group, such as the evaluation team, to and from their place of work each day. To assure appropriate arrangements it is desirable to have the visiting chairman view the proposed accommodations during his initial visit to the district several weeks before the evaluation.

VISITORS' ARRIVAL

It is best for the visiting evaluators to arrive during the late afternoon of the day prior to their first series of observations in the schools. The chairman of the self-evaluation should meet them at a previously agreed upon place, usually the superintendent's office or the motel itself. If the former, each evaluator, after being greeted by the superintendent and his immediate staff, should soon be directed to the motel so that he becomes familiar with its location and his accommodations. Prior to dinner the chairman of the visiting team will want to have a meeting with his group members. Their tasks and responsibilities will be outlined at this time. Administrators and self-evaluation committee members may be asked to be present either to clarify or elaborate on the self-evaluation report. Inquiries may also be made concerning other background materials that were previously furnished to each of the visiting educators.

"KICK-OFF" DINNER

The dinner that same evening serves a special purpose. It is the "kick-off" session where everyone concerned with the elementary schools' evaluation gets acquainted and hears initial presentations of procedural highlights. Board of Education members, the school district's administrators, the elementary schools' faculty, and PTA presidents are part of this gathering. Municipal government officials such as the mayor and council members may also be invited in some districts. The head table may include the chairman of the visiting evaluators, the superintendent of the district, the chairman of the self-evaluation, the president of the Board of Education, the president of the PTA federation and the mayor. In order to expedite each evaluator's acquaintance with a cross-section of the groups represented at the dinner it is wise to have a comprehensive selection of people at each table. Each visiting evaluator may be seated with, let us say, a school administrator, a PTA president, a municipal official, a subject-matter specialist, an upper grade teacher and a primary school instructor. If possible each table should include one individual who has been a chairman of a self-evaluation study group. This arrangement is conducive to the visitor's learning about the district from the vantage points enjoyed by persons holding a variety of positions in the school community. This plan provides a foundation for the free, friendly, cooperative attitude of the participants in all of their later contacts.

After being introduced and welcomed, the chairman of the visitors will provide introductory remarks concerning the purposes, procedures and benefits of the evaluation. The superintendent and the president of the Board of Education may also wish to speak briefly about the value of the assessment process the district is about to experience. Also pertinent is a synopsis of the self-evaluation process outlined by the chairman of that now-accomplished enterprise.

GUIDELINES FOR THE OBSERVERS

After breakfast of the first full day in the district each evaluator goes into the schools equipped with a general list of guidelines and a specific schedule for his activities. Both had been discussed by the team chairman at their first session held immediately after their arrival. A typical set of guidelines for the visiting evaluators would include the following:

1. Be constantly aware that your observations become the foundation for our evaluation. Look carefully, listen acutely and be certain of the facts. Check and recheck when necessary to assure your complete understanding of an objective, activity or administrative procedure. Take appropriate notes and do so immediately so that later, recall is more easily achieved.

2. Stay cognizant of the fact that our evaluative judgements are based upon the school district's philosophy of education represented by selected criteria. This community has exercised its right to set educational goals and objectives suited to their purposes. The evaluative instrument is our guide for the task of deciding how closely they approach these aims. Refrain from introducing your personal sets of values. We are to measure with the school system's yardstick.

3. Unobtrusiveness is to be practiced at all times. Enter classrooms with little comment, be seated as inconspicuously as possible and concentrate on observation. Do not participate in class discussions. Refrain from the temptation to provide correction or elaboration of any topic under consideration. If asked for opinion be courteously non-committal.

4. During discussion with staff do not feel free to make on-the-spot suggestions for improvement. Do not be critical. Our evaluation will be a team effort with our recommendations resulting from total membership consideration of the collected data.

5. Freely discuss your observations with your fellow evaluators. Solicit the results of their viewing a situation that you also have observed. Aid each other with establishing a proper alignment of your perceptions with the criteria standards. Consult with your chairman whenever a point of inquiry arises.

EVALUATOR'S AGENDA

In addition to guidelines for each observer it is beneficial for the evaluator to have a specific agenda. This schedule provides for the visitor to be "at the right place at the right time," so to speak. A creation of the team's chairman, it is prepared after his review of all of the schools' daily schedules for the days of the evaluation. A typical evaluator's agenda for a day of observation would be as follows:

OBSERVATION SCHEDULE – Tuesday, November 12

Evaluator: Mr. Walter Hamil
Area of Specialization: Reading

8:00 a.m.	Team Conference – Motel Meeting Room
8:30	Arrive Taylor School
	Meet Administrators – Conference Room
	Mr. Richard Wyhte, Principal
	Mr. Samuel Bodd, Vice-Principal
9:00	Visit Classroom – Kindergarten, Room 2
	Miss Barbara Codel
9:30	Visit Classroom – 1st grade, Room 5
	Mrs. Eleanor Waverly
10:00	Visit Classroom – 2nd grade, Room 7
	Mrs. Grace Widmer
10:30	Return to Conference Room
	Coffee Break
10:45	Visit Multi-Media Center
	Director Mrs. Viola Kampel
	Assistant Director Miss Janet Rigen
11:15	Visit Supplemental Reading Class
	Reading Specialist Miss Mary Salow
11:45	Lunch – With the School's Administrators in the Cafeteria
12:45	Visit Classroom – 3rd grade, Room 10
	Mrs. Julia Zum
1:15	Visit Classroom – 4th grade, Room 13
	Miss Karen Watson
1:45	Visit Classroom – 5th grade, Room 15
	Mr. Theodore Morgan
2:15	Visit Classroom – 6th grade, Room 18
	Mr. Gary Potter
2:45	Principal's Office
	Conference with administrators and reading specialist
3:15	Library
	Informal faculty and evaluators gathering
4:15	Return to Motel Meeting Room for Team Conference

The time given to an evaluation and the number of schools in the district are factors that would alter each evaluator's daily agenda. When a school district has many schools there must be enough evaluators so that each one of them spends a minimum of a half day in each building. This is not preferred, however, to the suggested visit of one day per school for each visiting assessor. In the observation schedule of Mr. Walter Hamil, seen above, it may be argued that the observer cannot see his area of assigned evaluation responsibility, reading, being taught in each of the classrooms he visits. The school authorities and the chairman of the outside team must come to an agreement about this matter. One solution is to have regular classroom schedules modified during the evaluation visits so that, in this case, reading activities would be taking place when the observer reaches each class. This adapting must be worked out prior to the evaluator's visit for each teacher involved must know of her modified schedule early enough for her to plan her day accordingly. Another way to approach the situation is not to be concerned about the observer seeking his specific area of interest taught in every classroom during each of his visitations. Rather, the regular school schedule is left untouched and while he sees his specialty taught in some classes, he notes in others the provision for its teaching, the materials and equipment available for its implementation and the kind of environment provided for its presentation. Also he may particularly seek to discuss the subject with those teachers who were not engaged with its instruction during his visit to their classrooms. That opportunity is offered to him during the after-school gathering of the evaluators and the school's faculty.

Another evaluator's daily agenda may look quite different when his assigned area of specialty is not subject-matter oriented. A typical schedule for an evaluator of a school's physical plant would be as follows:

OBSERVATION SCHEDULE, WEDNESDAY, MARCH 3

Evaluator: Mr. Henry Middleton
Area of Specialization: School Physical Plant

8:00 a.m.   Team Conference — Motel Meeting Room
8:30   Arrive Brighton School
            Meet Administrators — Teachers Room
                Mr. Joseph Parruci, Principal
                Mr. Timothy Conklin, Vice-Principal
9:00   Conference with Superintendent of Buildings
                Mr. Jason Worte
9:30   Tour of plant heating facilities, storage areas and custodial and maintenance rooms
10:30   Return to Teachers Room
            Coffee Break
10:45   Tour of outside grounds: play areas, parking zones and all approaches to the school
11:45   Lunch — With Superintendent of Buildings in the Cafeteria
12:45   Tour Classrooms, Rooms 1 – 18
2:15   Visit Library
                Miss Mildred Gary, Librarian
2:45   Visit All-Purpose Room

3:15   Conference with school custodians in custodians' room
         Mr. Charles White, Head Custodian
         Mr. George Pitt, General Custodian
3:45   Join informal faculty and evaluators gathering in Library
4:15   Return to Motel meeting room for Team Conferences

THE PRELIMINARY REPORT

One might ask how the chairman of the visiting evaluation team can effectively provide a report to the school system's personnel after only a few days in the district. It is true that at this gathering, held just before the visitors leave, the accounting of observed evidence, both pro and con, cannot be given in great depth. Rather, this preliminary report has as its purpose the revelation of initial impressions gained by the evaluators as they measured their observations against the evaluative criteria. It may be that their chairman will commend the schools for a program that takes full advantage of the present design of the physical plant. He may be able to praise the rapport the observers consistently encountered between administration and staff. Other typical first reporting might be in reference to the inadequacy of the library in its attempt to serve as a multi-media center or the instances related by the evaluators where the classroom facilities gave little opportunity for the teacher to work with individuals and small groups. Certainly at this time it is appropriate for the chairman, on behalf of his entire team, to thank those responsible for the courtesies extended to them throughout their visit. Further, it should be made clear that this oral report now being made is in no way complete and that it will be followed by a detailed written report that will be made available to all interested parties.

POST-EVALUATION SESSIONS

The evaluation team's work is not yet over. Once removed from the scene of observation the chairman, often with a selected deputy or two, must gather the collected data and place them in a logical, sequential form for presentation to the evaluated district. The basic question to be answered is how the observations of the visitors revealed the district in light of its philosophy and the selected evaluative criteria. Full reports need be made for each category that underwent scrutiny. While some chairmen do this alone, others seek the aid of a few key team members to join them as a committee in the writing enterprise.

Once rough drafts of the final report have been drawn the chairman calls a meeting of the entire team. Obviously, the most centrally located gathering spot is desirable because the members are usually from diverse, sometimes widely scattered areas. If it proves too difficult for the total team to meet as a unit, the chairman may call two separate meetings at different locations. One may be convenient for those from one geographical area and another may serve well for those from a different region.

During these post-evaluation meetings the team members are given the opportunity to review the total report and, most especially, their specific areas that were assigned to them during their visit. Suggested additions and deletions can be made at this time. Assuming the chairman and his writing committee have included the data into the first draft of a comprehensive report document, the team ought to make its modifications for its refinement known at one gathering.

The mechanics of preparing the printed version of the evaluation report can be the responsibility of the chairman with the evaluated school district reimbursing his expenses for the process. Another alternative is to have the chairman send the contents of the final report to the school system for their preparation of the document into multiple copies. Either way it is necessary that consideration be given to the production of a quantity that will satisfy the needs of both the school system and the community it serves. Also, each outside team member should be sent a completed copy for their future reference.

THE CHAIRMAN RETURNS TO THE DISTRICT

The evaluation team chairman culminates the activities of the visiting observers by reappearing in the school district when the final report is ready for distribution. At this time he has the opportunity to meet with the local board of education and summarize his team's findings to them as well as providing answers to their questions about his group's conclusions. Also he can meet with the district's administrators, giving them the benefit of his involvement in the evaluation process relating particularly as to how the findings affect their role of leadership in the district. Finally, he would meet with the total school staff and provide them with a synopsis of the outside observers' research in the system. This is a prelude to the valuable experience of reviewing recommendations and making decisions that lead to their implementation. Those activities will, of course, involve school personnel frequently after the formal evaluation and its reporting have been completed.

SUMMARY

The procedure of following a school system's self-evaluation with a formal visit of outside evaluators is a necessity for an unbiased, comprehensive view of the status of the schools. Getting this process operative takes planning and knowledge of a step-by-step sequence of activities if the enterprise is to be successful. This chapter sought to provide such direction.

Prior to the visit of the outside team to the school district it is wise to have preliminary conferences between the chairman of the visitors and local school officials. Usually the chairman of the district's self-evaluation is the key person for the host system. Typical of an agenda that would be devised through this cooperative endeavor is the schedule provided here.

AGENDA FOR VISITING EVALUATORS

Tuesday, March 4

4:30 p.m.	Check in at motel
5:30	Initial conference of team — Motel meeting room
6:30	Dinner at High School Cafeteria
7:30	Greetings — District Superintendent
	Mayor
	Chairman of Self-Evaluation Committee
	Remarks — Chairman of Visiting Team
8:30	Organizational meeting of team — High School Conference Room
10:30	Adjournment

Wednesday and Thursday, March 5 and 6

7:00 a.m.	Breakfast at motel
8:00	Team Conference — motel meeting room
8:30	Each evaluator arrives at assigned school
9:00	Observations made and conferences held as assigned to each evaluator
11:45	Lunch — as listed in individual agendas
12:45	Observations made and conferences held as assigned
3:15	Informal gathering of faculty and evaluators
4:15	Team Conference — motel meeting room
5:15	Rest period
6:30	Dinner at motel
7:30	Meetings of sub-committees
8:30	Total team conference
10:15	Adjournment

Friday, March 7

	Same as Wednesday and Thursday from 7:00 a.m. to 2:45 p.m.
2:45	Team conference meeting — Board of Education Conference Room
4:00	Gathering of total faculty and evaluators in school auditorium — Preliminary report by Chairman of Evaluation Team
5:00	Adjourn
5:30	Check-out of evaluators from motel

A "kick-off" dinner serves as an excellent vehicle for the evaluators to become acquainted with local school and community people. This gathering provides a good foundation for the contacts of the visitors with their hosts during the next few days of observation.

Each evaluator must be guided by elementary rules of observational conduct. Basic are

1. Observe carefully; be certain of your facts.
2. Be constantly aware that all judgements are based on observable evidence measured against local philosophy and evaluative criteria.
3. Refrain from classroom participation.
4. Be reluctant to pronounce on-the-spot cures for the district's ills.
5. Seek the consultation of your chairman and evaluating colleagues.

The act of observation is best carried out when each evaluator has a precise agenda designating his presence at activities pertinent to his inquiry. These schedules should provide direction from his first morning team meeting through visits to the schools through to the final late evening summation with his researching partners.

Important, of course, are the discussions that each assessor has with the school officials who are responsible in those areas being assessed. Equally valuable are the many informal talks held with all staff members during the after-school gatherings of evaluators and local personnel.

The chairman of the outside team provides the district with an oral preliminary report before the evaluators depart. Later, the group gathers at an agreed upon meeting area to review the first draft of the final report that has been prepared by the chairman and his writing committee. Copies are sent to the school district and the chairman reports in person to the Board of Education, administrative leaders, and the school staff giving highlights of the evaluation document.

7

Reporting the Findings
of the Team

When the evaluation process is finished, then a host of new problems face the faculty and school administration. What is the next step? Who gets the results of the evaluation? Do we report the whole series of commendations and recommendations or do we edit them? Should only school personnel get the entire report or should the Board of Education, Superintendent, Mayor, PTA officers also receive copies? The list of questions is unlimited.

ENTIRE REPORT AVAILABLE

Many of these questions should have been answered in advance of the evaluation process when the initial determination was made to evaluate the elementary school. For example, it is generally good practice to have as system philosophy the honest and complete reporting of the entire proceedings whenever an evaluation is undertaken by either the staff itself or by an outside visiting team. The same procedure would follow whenever a citizens' committee or an architect, or a state department official makes reports about the schools. If the report is too voluminous for dissemination of the entire report, then at least copies of the full report should be available for public perusal. This fact should be repeatedly stressed so that no one feels that anything is being hidden. Copies of the report can easily be placed in the library, school office, municipal office or wherever it could be easily read without undue effort.

WERE EVALUATION AIMS ACHIEVED?

The first step should be to examine the report to see if the aims and purpose of the evaluation were achieved by the evaluation study. If the purpose of the evaluation was narrow and limited to only study the effectiveness of the new arithmetic textbooks, then this purpose and this purpose only should be sought in the report of the evaluation study. The study should not concern itself only with reading scores, handwriting, health habits, social interrelationships or other broad areas of concern. On the other hand, if the study was not limited, and the objectives were broad, and the total school program and process were to be examined, then the final report should be equally comprehensive.

It may develop that the hoped for end result cannot be achieved because the criteria were not germane or do not supply the necessary data to enable the evaluation team to make specific determinations. It is also possible that the visiting committee may not do a thorough job. This could be the result of insufficient time, a poor committee, ineffective leadership, or simply not utilizing the evaluation criteria in a professional manner, However, all these possibilities are usually not found in practice and most of the evaluation teams operate in a truly competent manner.

UN-MET, NEW NEEDS REVEALED

A very common result of the evaluation by an outside group is not that many of the reported needs were supported by the study but that many new needs were uncovered or discovered. The same results occur in reference to the limitations that the faculty noted. New limitations will often be uncovered by the study group. These new discoveries will be of great interest to the administration and the Board of Education.

ORAL REPORT AT CONCLUSION OF EVALUATION

When the committee or visiting team completes its report, the results should be given to the staff of the school(s) concerned in the study. This is usually done orally by the chairman of the evaluation group. This report may only discuss the highlights of both recommendations and commendations. Questions and answers are not usually part of this final report. The complete written report should be received within a reasonable time of four to six weeks.

The organization and scope of the evaluation study will have a vital effect on the dissemination of the final report. If the study was of a single school, undertaken by the principal and staff for their own distinctly single school purpose, then the final report may go no further than the faculty of the school. Yet even in this very narrow gauge example, the final results may be of such a nature that others may need to be informed. For example, if the final result indicates a school and faculty need to convert the school from a typical self-contained school into a non-graded organization then the Superintendent or some central office personnel may need to become involved.

PRINCIPALS, CENTRAL OFFICE NOTIFIED OF EVALUATION RESULTS

Good professional practice will insure, whatever the result of a single school evaluation, that those results be at least the topic of a report to the other fellow administrators (if there be any) and to the central office. If the final report, for example, contained suggestions that teaching techniques such as the lecture system be reduced and more pupil initiated dialogue takes place, there may need be no further assistance from the central office. Yet once again, the faculty may feel that to truly understand this technique, workshops must be held. If building autonomy exists for the expenditure of funds allotted to the building, then this suggestion need not be approved elsewhere. But, if funds are not so allocated, then the central office must become involved in the final report, if the results are to be implemented. The same reasoning applies to suggestion for new materials, equipment, and supplies where the vital ingredient in fulfilling the recommendation is the availability of funds.

If the evaluation study was of many or all of the elementary schools in a district, then the final report assumes a status of great proportion. Not only will the individual school faculty be concerned, but the faculties, the administrators, the parents of the schools, the central office administration, the board of education, and the entire community. The condition of the schools, the reasons for the evaluation, the dynamics of the community situation will all influence the receptivity of the final report. If the schools are well supported, well regarded and no special problems exist, then it is likely that the report will be calmly received by all concerned. If on the other hand, the schools are in an uproar over some special condition that evaluation is to consider, then the community and school groups will most probably be at least apprehensive not only about the results of the final report, but the dissemination of that report.

DISSEMINATION OF FINAL REPORT OF VITAL IMPORTANCE

The dissemination of the final report therefore is a matter of great importance. It will condition the acceptance of the recommendations and provide a support for the truthfulness of the commendations. Not only must the school community but the community at large must feel that the entire report is available. Both groups need absolute assurance that nothing is being hidden or "covered up."

PTA NOTIFIED OF EVALUATION RESULTS

In addition to the reports to the other administrators, the Parent-Teacher group should also be informed of the results of the evaluation. Many of the evaluation plans for the elementary school will have sections for the inclusion of parents in the evaluation process. Parents will welcome a part in the evaluation process and will eagerly cooperate with the staff. The more involved the community is in the evaluation process the more they should be involved in the final dissemination of the results of the evaluation. This very important group should have been informed all along of the decision to do the evaluation, the reasons for the evaluation, and the objectives of the evaluation. Assuming this to be the process of communication as the evaluation was proceeding, then at least the executive committee of the PTA should be informed of the results of the evaluation. The nature of the final results may require the calling of a special meeting of the PTA to hear the final report. It is possible that the individual school will have other groups besides the PTA that will be interested in the evaluation findings. These groups may be either civic, religious, or political in nature. The faculty and building principal will know these groups and can help determine the extent and involvement of them in the dissemination of the final report.

STUDENTS SHOULD BE INFORMED OF RESULTS

Another very important group that needs to be considered in the final dissemination process are the students of the school(s). Once again, it should be part of the evaluation process that the students be informed that the faculty is considering the evaluation of the school and the reasons for that evaluation. This explanation must be tailored to the level of understanding of the particular student and be couched in terms that he can comprehend. The students must not be ignored; they must not be forgotten by saying that this is a professional matter for teachers and administrators only. The students are capable of understanding and will appreciate knowing that their school is trying to better itself. It is likely that they may wish to have something to say or they may even want to be a part of the evaluation process. Elementary pupils can be a fruitful part of the evaluation undertaking if serious thought is given the part they are to take in this vital school process. If they have been part of the evaluation procedure then they must have part in the final dissemination of results.

The central office will usually determine the extent of involvement of teachers in the other buildings, the other administrators and the Board of Education. These decisions are usually not a function of the individual school where the evaluation was made. However, the school faculty should know that these other groups are to be informed of the results of the evaluation of their school. This is but a common courtesy that is too often forgotten. It is possible that individual members of the faculty will be asked to assist in the presentation of parts of the final report to one or another of these groups. The building principal will normally be involved in public presentations to whatever group is present.

DIFFERENT POINTS OF EMPHASIS

A most important thought to be considered in the meetings with the various groups that will hear the final report is the point of emphasis that will be made to each group. All groups will not be equally interested in the same parts of the evaluation. One group may be concerned with building needs, classroom space and future building plans. Another group may be interested in the report of standardized test scores, or reading levels in the various grades. A third group may focus on the extent of participation of private or parochial children in the Federal programs. It is possible that the PTA will want to become involved in all of the recommendations. Although the interests of each group are somewhat predetermined, nevertheless, all parts of the report should be made available if the group so wishes. It would destroy the confidence of the group in the entire report if parts of the report were not made available to them.

The report to the Board of Education will normally be made by the Superintendent or by a member of the Central Staff. Usually the full evaluation report will be given to the Board members. If the report is very lengthy, a summary of the recommendations and commendations may only be distributed to the Board members. The Board of Education will usually make the decision for the distribution of the final report to members of the municipal governing body and to the state officials.

PROBLEMS OF PROCESS OF DISSEMINATION

Once the decisions are made as to which groups are to receive the final report of the evaluatiion study then a new problem arises, namely the process of that dissemination. What media is to be used—word of mouth, school newspaper, formal meetings, school district newsletter, local or regional newspaper, radio, television? The response to these questions leads to the next question—who shall perform the above tasks? The answers to these questions then lead to the next logical questions—when and where shall these events occur?

A quick obvious answer to the above inquiries is—use all the methods and media that are possible, use any person who can assist meaningfully, and do all these things as soon as possible after the final report is received.

A standard textbook on public relations will outline most of the usual methods of the use of media, the various "publics" that may be affected, and the typical programming of these events. The suggestions that follow that are related to the dissemination of the final evaluation report are therefore somewhat brief with only the highlights mentioned.

Group	Person(s)	Topic	Media	Timing
School Faculty	Self-Study Chairman Committee Chairman Principal	Final Results	Talk	Conclusion of evaluation (study)
Other Administrators	Principal	Final Results	Talk Transparencies	Soon after conclusion of evaluation (study)
Other Teachers	Principal Self-Study Chairman	Summary Final Results Recommendations Commendations	Talk Transparencies	Soon after conclusion of evaluation (study) or when new group is ready to start
PTA Executive Committee	Principal Self-Study Chairman	Final Results Commendations Recommendations	Talk	Very soon after conclusion of evaluation (study)
PTA general or special meeting	Principal Self-Study Chairman	Final Results Commendations Recommendations	Talk Transparencies	Soon after evaluation (study) is completed

Group	*Person(s)*	*Topic*	*Media*	*Timing*
Superintendent Central Staff	Principal	Final, complete report	Talk/Discussion Full written Report	Immediately after conclusion evaluation (study)
Students	Principal Faculty	Final Results	Talk/Discussion	Soon after eval uation (study) is completed
Board of Edu- cation	Superintendent	Highlights of Commendations Recommendations	Talk/Discussion	First meeting after conclusion of evaluation (study)
Municipal Offi- cials	Superintendent Board of Education President	Highlights Recommendations Commendations	Full Written Report or precis of report	After the Administration PTA, and Board of Education have been informed
General Public	Superintendent Public Relations Chairman Central Staff	Final Results	Radio, TV Newspapers District News- letter	Very soon after conclusion of evaluation (study)
General Staff	Superintendent Central Staff	Highlights Final Results	Intra-Staff Bulletin	Soon after conclusion of evaluation (study)

One Half Year Later

Repeat most of previous suggestions.
Highlight positive steps taken.

One Year Later

Repeat most of previous suggestions.
Highlight positive *results* accruing
from study.

BOARD OF EDUCATION CONSIDERS ITEMS THAT NEED POLICY DECISIONS

Each group involved in the final dissemination of the evaluation report will naturally emphasize the material that is of greatest concern to them. They may ignore or at least not stress other items. For example, the board of education should deal only with those items that require policy decisions, leaving items that are operational in nature for the administration and faculty to stress. The final report may state that more audio-visual aids are needed for each classroom and recommend that one television set, one super-eight movie camera and projector, etc., be supplied for each room. In addition, the finding might indicate that the present equipment be better utilized by the staff. The first suggestion would properly be a matter for board of education on policy consideration, since it would have implications for the entire system and would require large outlays of money. The second part would be a matter for the building principal to overcome.

ALL ITEMS OF FINAL REPORT TO BE DISCUSSABLE

The PTA group would naturally be concerned with such matters as the quality of the teaching staff, the level of individualization of instruction, the ego-development and ego-nourishment that the school provides for each student. They may also wish to make their voices heard about matters such as the audio-visual materials when the school budget is being considered. Also, they may want to express a viewpoint about an item such as staff turnover, with all the implications that item has for salary schedules, and school budgets. What is being stressed is that although each group may seem to have clearly delineated areas of concern, in actual practice the lines are not clearly drawn and any group may wish to be heard on any item of the evaluation. This point of view should be encouraged, and constant stress made that the whole report is available, is discussable, and is of concern to the whole district and any attempt to restrict information or discussion will result in suspicion, and reduce the impact of the final report.

The staff might be interested in items that will make their teaching more effective, such as the supplying of multiple text material, more paperback books, additional in-service training in specific areas. They may perhaps focus on items that were the subject of negotiations with the board of education such as more paraprofessionals or more assistance to supervise the playgrounds at lunchtime. The staff usually shows great professionalism about the various recommendations for school improvement. The extent of this can usually be anticipated by the professionalism shown in the self-study. If this was seriously performed, then the final reports will also be equally considered.

STUDENT INTEREST HIGH ABOUT EVALUATION RESULTS

Many would think that the students would have interest in only those items of the evaluation that are recreational in nature. Experience has shown, however, that the students have a wide and far-reaching interest in many other phases of the school. They take very seriously such matters as needed equipment for instruction, particularly the audio-visual machines that are integrated into the study carrels, and machines that assist the pupil in self-instruction. The students will also be interested in needed physical facilities both indoor and outdoors, in comments about student involvement and participation in the operation of the school or in the supplementary instruction of other pupils. The faculty and administration will find the student body to be one of their most avid "groups" studying the report. The faculty and administration have the responsibility to involve the students both before and after the evaluation in a meaningful and responsible way.

It is the obligation of the administration primarily to see to it that the interdependence and interrelatedness of the evaluation recommendations and commendations are made clear to the various groups. This should not be left to chance; it should be carefully planned and organized in advance of dissemination of the report.

SIDE BENEFITS OF EVALUATION

When the suggestions for dissemination of the final report are carried out, side benefits not directly related to the evaluation itself will accrue that may not be anticipated. The benefits of a thorough and complete dissemination of the evaluation report are many. All the groups mentioned will feel that they have been informed, that there is a spirit of openness, that nothing is too sacred to discuss, that the evaluation report is important, that all items will receive serious consideration, that the welfare of the students and the school are being given real emphasis, that improvement is desired, and that the opinions of the total community are being sought to this end.

ESPRIT DE CORPS

As these procedures are being carried out, some other results will occur that will be of great importance. A feeling of cohesiveness among the staff should be apparent by the end of the study. They will have worked together in a truly professional cause for not only their own benefit but for the children in their care. This sense of togetherness that their students display when they do meaningful work will also hold true for the faculty. To the extent that the students are involved they will also have these same feelings.

SENSE OF PURPOSE

A sense of purpose will also be present for all concerned who have been part of the team that helped to set the tone and direction of the school. The honest look, the careful appraisal, the professional examination of the school by the staff will leave not only the staff but also the parents with a feeling of a thorough, impartial examination having been made. From this there should follow respect for having performed this task for their children. Most persons sense the difficulty of self-study, of self-examination, and know the agony and effort it takes to do this. It may be that this is all that is needed to lift the parents and community to a new and more significant level of understanding, and of support of their schools. There may come about a new awareness of the problems and of the possible solutions to these problems that the schools face.

BENEFITS OF EVALUATION

Pupils	Teachers	Principals	Superintendent	Board of Education	Parents	Community
Improve school program and climate	Esprit de Corps	Objective appraisal of school	Have needs of schools analyzed subjectively and objectively	Objective basis for new policy considerations	Teachers sincerely trying to improve education for their children	Receive an objective review of school's progress and results
Impressed that they are involved	Sense of cohesiveness	Opportunity to examine school in depth	Basis for district improvement identified	Accurate data for budget needs	Objective review of their school by outside group	Know schools are open to suggestions and criticisms
Informed of school(s) desire to improve	Sense of purpose	Show openness to critical look at school	Material for budget compilation disclosed	Gain unbiased look at school's strength and weakness	Subjective review of their school by their teachers	See analysis of school system's needs by impartial outside group
Shown by example that one's strengths and weakness can be examined in a non-threatening way	True professionalism	Exert leadership with different groups	Total picture of schools revealed	Assess policies that influenced commendations	Work cooperatively to obtain recommendations	Preview of economic results of evaluation
Participants in a true-to-life relevant learning situation	Relevant Work	Grow professionally	Clues gained for policy recommendations	Show community that improvement is desired	Opportunity to discuss philosophy and purpose of school	Assure that tax funds are meaningfully expended
	Self-analysis	Basis for improvement identified	Gain perspective of school(s)			
	Work examined critically by others	Satisfaction gained from commendations	Willingness to have leadership results examined			
	Satisfaction gained for commended items	Priority needs established	Assess school direction and growth			
	Shown by example as well as precept that one's work can be examined in a non-threatening way	Furnishes material for an analysis of strengths and weaknesses	Spirit of self-analysis appraisal embraced by administrators and teachers			
		Discover areas for improvement not presently perceived				

171

INTERDEPENDENCE OF GROUPS TO IMPLEMENT RESULTS

If the interrelatedness of the various items is clearly pointed out, then the interdependence of the various groups to implement the report should be made equally clear. Ideally then, cooperation and understanding would flow from the faculty to the community and from community back to the faculty. This hoped for "utopian" goal must be sought for, planned for, and worked for—it will not "just" happen.

PRICE TAG ON RECOMMENDATIONS

The economics of the evaluation report will normally be only partially grasped by the individual school faculty. It is usually the job of the principal or the central administration staff to put a price tag on the various recommendations of the report. The implications of individual recommendation are not always clear to the school faculty. If they wish to have more playground supervision assistance in accordance with the final evaluation study, this might first of all become a matter for the negotiation process and something that cannot be decided by an individual administrator. It might also become a matter for the board of education since all the other schools will want the same new benefit. The difficulty of securing the recommendations that were suggested by the final report must be made clear to all the various groups so that they do not accuse either the administration or the board of education of not taking the recommendation seriously.

ORDER OF PRIORITY OF RECOMMENDATIONS

Once the price tag is put on the various suggestions and recommendations of the final report then an order of priority must be placed on the items. Some items will need immediate attention and should be corrected at once. Other material can be programmed for the next year's budget, while still others can be postponed for one or two years. There will also be some suggestions that the faculty and administration will not agree with. There should be no hesitation about disagreeing with individual recommendations if care is taken to insure that sufficient time and study are given to the item. Great care should be taken with the disputed items. The staff and general public will want full explanations and a showing of full and fair analysis of the item.

MUNICIPAL OFFICIALS AND PARENTS CAN HELP IMPLEMENT RECOMMENDATIONS

In some instances the economic picture of recommendations will depend upon the state or federal government for funds. If this be so, then the presentation of this fact should be coupled with suggestions for obtaining those funds. This will be the usual responsibility of the superintendent or the board of education. The municipal officials may be of assistance in this respect and their aid should be sought. If the particular state or federal program is one that may be influenced by petitions from the parents, then this help should also be requested. Past practice has shown that the municipal officials and the parents are eager to assist in matters of this kind. They wish to have their voices heard and to feel that they have some influence. Their participation will also help them to more fully understand all the ramifications and implementing recommendations of the final evaluation report. New or pilot programs that require large sums or that are of long term action are examples. Other illustrations are those programs that need cooperation with other school districts whether within or without the state. The final report will contain much material about the specific or total community that may be new information to the staff and the community itself. Such statistics as the school evaluation criteria requires will not typically be part of the general knowledge of the community. The average income, the classification of employment of the wage earners, the number of homes, the educational attainment of the adults, dollars back of each pupil, and average number of children per family, are but some of the examples.

The report may also give a new perspective on the socio-economic levels of the school community or the ethnic makeup of the school children and parent group.

ALL RECOMMENDATIONS SHOULD BENEFIT PUPILS

One very common and excellent outcome of the evaluation process that should be quite clear in the final report is that the school is truly trying to better the education provided for the students. In fact, all the recommendations should give as their end point the improvement of education for the school children. This point should be constantly present in all the end results of the study. The philosophy of the school and the school system will also be quite in evidence all throughout the evaluation but never more evident than in the final recommendations. These end suggestions must keep in mind the starting point, the purpose and thrust of the individual school, so that the recommendations all aim at furthering this philosophy. If some of the suggestions are in conflict with the stated philosophy of the school, then this must be carefully pointed out. Once again, it will be noted that the aim and objectives of the school, and the process of carrying out that purpose will come under scrutiny, even at the very end of the study.

SUMMARY

The examination of the final recommendations by all concerned will furnish a marvelous opportunity for the community to do some cooperative planning, to make a genuine examination of the school where their children attend, a chance to perhaps make some improvements for the betterment of the school either in a material or subjective sense, to focus for at least a brief period of time on the school, to learn what a group of teachers can suggest as a result of their own self-study, to benefit by an objective appraisal of the school by an objective outside professional evaluation team, to know that improvement of education in that school for their children is being seriously considered, and to feel hope that positive good results will accrue, to give the community a chance to participate in a review of the school direction and growth, to make the students know by example that they can have a part in the assessment of their school, and to show the community that the schools are open for suggestions and criticisms.

8

Reaping the Benefits
of Evaluation

Appraisal of any school, we have suggested, needs to follow three steps. The first of these is the pre-evaluation process employed by the staff concerned. This initial activity more often than not strongly supports the desirability of step two, a formal evaluation process conducted by an outside professional team. The third step, the post-evaluation activities, offers opportunities to implement both the practical and philosophical recommendations of evaluation. Post-evaluation is a *process* that facilitates the study of a team's findings, recommendations and conclusions with an eye to precipitate action. All the aspects and facets of corrective action are examined in step three, i.e., the formulation of school goals, planning of stratagems for the attainment of those goals, full consideration of available and needed staff and material resources, establishment of specific policies and administrative decisions affecting instructional programs, services, budget, facilities and community needs as well as resolution of differences regarding the adequacy and judiciousness of those policies and decisions.

Self-help, stimulated and guided by the visiting team, is the ultimate objective of evaluation. The willingness to expose a school to impartial judgement would seem to imply the willingness to act upon that judgement. It has been observed that without this mature interpretation of evaluation intent, no more than superficial and virtually useless results are derived. No school or system should contemplate evaluation without total commitment to objective evaluation, follow-up and properly motivated corrective action. Our elementary schools are indeed under attack and only through well-conceived, well-planned, positive remedial action can we effectively resist unjust criticism and strengthen aspects of our programs which require improvement. The burden of responsibility our elementary schools carry certainly needs the kind of redistribution, of priorities if you will, that permits the actualization of the highest ideals without the undesirable hindrances that heretofore have been accepted. Americans have traditionally sought quality and economy. Why cannot we enjoy those highly desirable qualities in all our elementary schools?

ESTABLISHING PRIORITIES

One of the most difficult tasks confronting a school or school system immediately following evaluation is the ordering of priorities for change. A total evaluation usually generates findings, conclusions and recommendations that touch upon every aspect of educational theory and practice. Generally speaking, the more inclusive the evaluative instrument employed, the more productive and complex the yield of data requiring treatment. No single person or group can or should assume the right or responsibility for developing a schedule for effecting improvements. There will be monetary decisions to be made that will require board of education and community approvals. Instructional shortcomings will necessitate staff involvement and action. The administration, special service personnel, students and parents, among others, will likewise have thoughts bearing upon what (to them) represents a realistic, orderly progression toward a sound ordering of priorities.

Each segment of the school community will without doubt seek to concern itself with that portion of the evaluation report directly affecting its area of special interest. Such attention is wholesome and ought to be fostered and encouraged. Steps must be taken, however, to insure that the work carried on by any one group is not exclusive of the others. The board of education, administration and faculty must function interdependently. They must rely upon each other for support and endorsement if substantial improvement is to be forthcoming. It is with this realization in mind that we strongly recommend the formation of a representative council or committee to integrate the work of all interested parties. In many instances, the original self-evaluation committee has functioned well in this follow-up role. Some schools have preferred to choose an entirely new committee, one reflecting membership selected with due regard to special talents in the areas of discerned weakness.

BROAD BASE COMMITTEE

Whatever local factors influence the selection of persons to serve on a post-evaluation coordinating unit, it should be remembered that a broadly based representative group will offer increased opportunities to achieve more fully the sought after educational improvements. The role of this committee is to facilitate, expedite, coordinate and communicate. The charge to the committee should make clear the extent and nature of responsibilities assigned to the committee, as well as those reserved by law or mutual agreement to constituted bodies within the school or system unit.

GROWTH OF STAFF

The aspect of professional growth which serves to upgrade a teacher's classroom effectiveness is of the greatest significance. No other benefit or change can equal its importance. An improved pupil-teacher learning environment must remain the primary consideration and the ultimate goal of purposeful evaluation. Whenever this concern has been the major point of emphasis, teachers report that evaluation has:

1. encouraged wider use of teacher procedures which provide for the differences that individual pupils manifest in their rate and manner of cognitive development;
2. created an atmosphere in which greater participation by *all* pupils in the learning activities of the classroom was permitted;
3. increased staff consciousness of the need to establish and develop more effective communication at the pupil-pupil and teacher-pupil levels, both in and out of the classroom;
4. promoted better methods of questioning which employed more varied types and levels of difficulty designed to satisfy the needs of individual and different pupils;
5. established more clearly the importance of multi-media resources and provided insight into how these materials could and should be effectively used in the teaching situation;
6. provided the basis for understanding the need to give students opportunity to propose changes in both the format and direction of lesson content;
7. achieved increased teacher involvement in efforts directed toward reaching a deeper understanding of individual pupils and a desire to know more about one's students than is revealed by mere I.Q. or reading scores;
8. offered new options for the utilization of teaching time which realistically treat the individual skills and concept development of pupils who vary greatly in the time required to accomplish learning tasks;
9. enabled teachers to see the relationship between the school's educational philosophy and the on-going classroom activities with the accompanying realization that it is each teacher, as a member of the school's instructional team, who daily seeks to achieve the school's goals;
10. increased appreciation for and acceptance of the important contributions which self-evaluation makes to one's individual growth and professional development as a teacher.

IMPROVEMENT OF INSTRUCTION FOR PUPILS

Most of the findings, recommendations and conclusions arrived at by the self-study committees and the outside visiting team will relate directly to the need for improvement of one or more aspects of classroom instruction. The obsolescence of textbooks, lack of multi-sensory teaching materials, over-dependence upon workbooks and the failure to effectively individualize teaching, are a few examples of deficient conditions which may exist. While the first two deficiencies mentioned above might easily be resolved through increased expenditures for books and audio-visual aids, the last two items certainly require a more comprehensive approach to an effective solution. Too great reliance upon workbooks and overly structured classroom teaching are manifestations of a pedagogical illness that money transfusions, without accompanying therapy, cannot remedy.

For purposes of discussion and illustration let us cite several recommendations extracted from an actual evaluation team report. These recommendations reflect the need for one school district to improve one vital aspect of teaching, namely, the individualization of instruction.

Spelling and Handwriting

Recommendation: Grouping within a class was observed in one case. This permitted the unusually good spellers to move far ahead in the spelling text. Good! We recommend this practice. Where children have definite handwriting needs the teacher should plan work to meet these individual needs instead of placing a whole class in a writing text at the same level.

Reading

Recommendation: Independent work (seatwork) carried out while groups are reading with the teacher usually includes spelling, writing, or mathematics. Upon completion of this work children may choose the activity they want. A higher type of independent work should be planned, such as: creative writing (observed in a few rooms), recreational reading, use of a listening station, or viewing of related filmstrips.

Mathematics

Recommendation: The committee felt that more grouping by ability and achievement should be practiced in order to adapt instruction to the varying needs of individuals.

Obviously, more definitive data must be compiled before any action on such recommendations can be initiated. Is the individualization of instruction not being actualized because multi-level teaching materials are not available? Do teachers lack the necessary training in the management techniques prerequisite to carrying on individualized instruction? Has the total staff really accepted this concept and not merely given it tacit approval? What is the attitude of supervisors and administrators? Are there physical limitations in the classrooms which discourage individualized and/or small group work? Do the evaluation team's findings regarding individualization merit staff acceptance as an accurate, representative image of what is actually taking place in the classrooms?

COOPERATIVE CORRECTIVE ACTION

It has frequently been said that the truly demanding work of evaluation begins when all the results of the team's visitation have been submitted, collated, summarized and reported. It is at this point that the staff must, if maximum benefits are to be enjoyed, direct its energies to the difficult and time consuming task of probing for the causative factors of whatever instructional weaknesses may be revealed by the evaluation. A sequential program of corrective action by teachers and administrators must now be cooperatively developed. This activity must be guided by the overriding attitude of positiveness, taking great care not to fix the blame for shortcomings on any individuals or groups within the school or community. Such captious attempts only serve to undermine the entire evaluation enterprise by attributing political motives to the activity and seriously retarding the realization of the wholesome benefits which would otherwise be derived.

The findings, recommendations and conclusions contained in the report of an evaluation team can at best reflect the immediate judgements and considered professional opinions of well qualified individuals. These persons must, within the brief interval of two or three days, review and assess every aspect and facet of the complex, dynamic and living social agency that we call a "school." We must accept the fact that the evaluation report will be largely a reflection of symptomatic conditions diagnosed as present. In other words, the team will, indeed can only, report on what it reads, observes and hears. It cannot stop to identify, analyze and weigh all the causative factors that contribute to "things as they are." The team can and usually will offer helpful comment, suggest instructional refinements and indicate investigative needs. It is the local school or school district that must take its cues from these advisements offered by the team in its evaluation report. The team's suggestions offer sound logical bases for planning and implementing improvements in the learning environment.

Let us return briefly to the recommendations quoted above that concern the need for one school district to further individualize instruction in spelling, handwriting, reading and mathematics. We can attest to the fact that the district's personnel accepted those recommendations as the basis for an intensive post-evaluation critique. The results of this exploratory effort revealed:

1. the instructional staff did recognize and accept individualization of instruction as a highly desirable yet unfulfilled goal in many classrooms;
2. the supervisory and administrative personnel also realized the importance of individualization but readily admitted that their attempts to foster and promote this concept had met with only moderate success;
3. the supply of multi-level materials and texts was found to be more than adequate to facilitate the approach toward individualized instruction;
4. the physical facilities were conducive to individual and small group work within the classrooms, library and special purpose teaching stations.

What then were the reasons why individualization of instruction was not practiced as the rule rather than the exception? Through interviews, observations and further internal examination, the major hindrances were eventually isolated. All of the deterrents in this case were found to be part of what might generally be referred to as problems in "classroom management of techniques for individualization." Teachers were uncertain of procedures and methodology and wanted practical examples of individualization in the several subject areas. They sought assistance and advice directly related to their grade assignments and students' age levels. Generally, the teaching staff needed in-service training experiences that would provide the required methodology and encourage actual classroom experimentation with individualization of instruction.

A series of highly productive grade-level, in-service workshops were conducted. They were workshops designed to examine real needs. The planning was done by the teachers themselves. Though the in-service workshop approach is not the solution to all professional improvement problems, it did, in this situation, literally work wonders for the entire staff. The in-service workshop is perhaps the most widely employed method for effecting improved on-the-job performance. It is difficult to imagine an evaluation concluding without at least one subsequent in-service workshop. Unfortunately, many such workshops are poorly conceived and almost totally unproductive.

IN-SERVICE WORKSHOP PLANNING

If shortcomings revealed by the evaluation team are chosen as the subject of faculty workshops, allow us to recommend for your consideration the following "do's" and "don'ts" of workshop planning.

IN-SERVICE WORKSHOP PLANNING

1. Do gear the workshop to a program of action.
2. Do plan the workshop cooperatively with a representative group of participants.
3. Do consider unifying the workshop around a central theme or problem faced by the school district.
4. Do allow for flexibility and mobility. Remember that time schedules, weather conditions, changes in personnel participation are all factors that affect workshop plans. The effective workshop coordinator alters and adjusts his program to accommodate necessary change.
5. Do develop enough structure to the program so that participants feel secure.
6. Do seek concrete, specific and tangible results of the workshop. A wrap-up review of learnings is a most essential ingredient at the conclusion of any workshop.
7. Do have a brief introductory orientation period setting forth aims, purposes and procedures for the workshop. Be sure the action of the workshop is related to these stated objectives.
8. Do have available all the necessary materials to encourage experimentation.
9. Do insist on movable furniture and adequate spacing of tables and chairs. Special attention should be given to proper light control, ventilation and voice amplification.
10. Do have all participants evaluate the workshop. Such exploration will serve to refine and improve practices and procedures.

---

1. Don't permit the workshop to become too large. In the case of post-evaluation professional improvement workshops, participation should be limited to from 50 to 75 teachers.
2. Don't schedule several work groups in one room. Noise and movement associated with participation reduce effective thinking.
3. Don't develop a workshop plan using only constant intervals of time for each session. Vary the length of your work periods.
4. Don't expect that a single workshop experience will produce the solution to all of the problems considered.
5. Don't allow socializing to grow to the point that it substitutes for this important program of in-service education.
6. Don't crowd the schedule. Allow ample time for inquiries, discussions and informal exploration.
7. Don't over-emphasize any single point to the extent that the total message becomes obscure.
8. Don't spread workshop groups throughout a large building. Assign working groups to rooms near an auditorium or gymnasium where they may convene and reconvene with ease.
9. Don't interrupt or detract from the work sessions by making announcements which are unrelated to the workshop content. Try to make such announcements, if necessary, at the start or end of the workshop.
10. Don't fail to summarize in written form the results of the workshop and distribute same to all participants.

EVALUATION AND THE TREND TOWARD NEGOTIATION

No current treatment of school evaluation may be considered complete without some serious mention of the relationship between collective negotiation and the free exercise and conduct of the school evaluation activity. At all instructional levels, school evaluation is growing in importance as a most desirable vehicle for bringing about educational progress. At the same time, the trend toward collective negotiation moves forward on a sure course, one which is destined to meet head-on with the issues involved in the very processes and techniques of evaluation.

Evaluation presupposes a liberal degree of freedom and autonomy that is often incompatible with the constraints of some negotiated work contracts. We refer particularly to those contracts which have approached evaluation as a divisive issue rather than a matter of mutual concern for all parties. Whenever school evaluation has been managed in that way, there has been created an adversary proceeding. As a direct consequence, teachers and administrators have found themselves, not infrequently, on opposite sides of the bargaining table. In the heat of bargaining and under the most stressful conflict conditions, decisions that challenge the quality of the instructional program are rendered. Our long-standing resistance to the brand of bureaucratic domination that leads to conformity in our schools may well succumb to yet another kind of stifling control; the type that is inherent in the harsh labor-management confrontation. The new standards for schools could easily become the lowest common denominator arrived at in the most inferior work contracts negotiated. Searching self-appraisal cannot produce quality results when contracts are too limiting. Widespread, in-depth staff involvement is essential if self-evaluation is to be truly productive. Also, more teachers and administrators must work together in a genuine spirit of willing cooperation, disclosing every aspect of the school's operations for review by both the internal study committees and the visiting team. Conditions agreed to in the work contract must not be immune to the objective appraisal of the evaluators. To prohibit such freedom in assessment would seriously handicap the evaluation and would virtually eliminate comment and recommendations dealing with matters that pose a major threat to the vitality and well-being of the school.

There is no easy solution to the negotiation-evaluation dilemma. Surely, no single group is to be blamed for the present crisis. Local educational associations have not intentionally sought to curtail or eliminate evaluations. Isolated actions taken toward that end are either unwitting or shortsighted. Indeed, the professional goals of teachers are well served by evaluation since it offers increased staff involvement in policy and program decision making. Evaluation expands the role of teachers in the governance of the school and provides the catalyst for greater community response to pressing school needs.

In the final analysis it must be said that no party to negotiation: teachers, administrators, or boards of education, can be expected to subvert its group interests at the bargaining forum. However, some positive steps can and must be taken to safeguard the right to evaluate and the freedom to do so in an atmosphere of full acceptance. The following are offered, not as final solutions to complex problems, but rather as suggestions for some positive action in defense of evaluation.

1. Negotiators must keep the concerns of evaluation in the forefront of their thinking. Evaluation is of mutual importance and with all concerned attentive to its non-yielding and necessary conditions, unsound provisions may be denied incorporation into any work agreement.
2. When evaluation is accepted by all as being of mutual importance and its convincing merits are agreed upon, write its conditions into the contract. This action would both acknowledge the worth of evaluation and elevate it to the status of an enforceable, contractual stipulation.
3. The work contract may need to be reviewed as a result of the evaluation recommendations. However, this work contract review is not the function of the evaluation team, but is the responsibility of the parties to the negotiated agreement.

IMPROVED PERCEPTION OF SCHOOLS BY THE COMMUNITY

There is attached to an outside team's evaluation findings a certain aura of validity and reliability that singularly is associated with the work of authorities. The statements made by the team relative to the strengths and weaknesses discovered will prompt communities to view their schools in an entirely new light. At best, there will be created a general acceptance of the desirability of change. A new interest in schools will be evidenced at gatherings of the board of education, P.T.A., church, civic and fraternal organizations. The public's attention will be focused upon the evaluation report, and therefore, upon the real and pressing problems of the schools. Communities will experience a certain reassurance and considerable pride in an enumeration of the schools many attributes. There will be a united and genuine effort to get at the problem areas that detract from quality performance.

At worst, the team's findings could be resoundingly rejected by the community. Local pride might suffer a near fatal blow and the citizenry evidence a resentful attitude toward the "outside interference." Thoughtful and intelligent management of post-evaluation activities can, we have suggested, avoid any such negative overtones and establish a climate in which the greatest evaluation benefits may be reaped.

SUMMARY

Evaluation is the process that attempts to appraise the relative strengths and weaknesses of a single school or system as they pertain to curricula, staff and physical facilities. It is founded upon the basic premise that every component part of the school's or system's operation has relevance to the conditions which obtain and should therefore be subject to professional, periodic examination. Evaluation is diagnostic. However, the aims and purposes of evaluation go beyond any simple accounting of the strong and weak points. Unless the findings of an evaluation are translated into positive, corrective action, the effort will have been misspent and every potential benefit lost.

The procedures and outcomes of school evaluation represent real opportunities for a deliberate balance and sharing of the power to make decisions that affect the future function and purpose of the school. Those decisions touch the very lives and beliefs of every individual within the school community and consequently, the mere mention of impending evaluation inspires a powerful surge of interest and activity among the members of the administration, faculty, board of education and the general citizenry. It is clear that the definition of roles and responsibilities, as they encompass each constituent party, will be neither easy nor tranquil. However, to paraphrase Socrates, "the unexamined school is probably not worth having."

Appendix

How much better or worse off are today's schools operating a full decade after Sputnik I? What is the state of our schools in terms of what is taught and what is learned in all the various subjects and not just in the science and mathematics areas, alone? Is this not the principle issue and the major question to which we must address ourselves? Yet, there exists no definitive answer to this all important question. There is no way to refute with fact the mass of charges leveled at our schools, no manner of assuring ourselves that we have selected the "right" order of priorities for effecting needed changes in our schools. Such is the case, largely because there has never been, until this point in time, a general acceptance of the concept that a periodic nationwide assessment of our schools could foster improvement without severely damaging the essential form and fabric of the system. Indeed, within recent years proposals for nationwide evaluation have met with forceful opposition from both teacher and administrative groups. Proponents of a national review have only now won shaky agreement for a voluntary invitational assessment plan of limited scope and character. The opposition to national assessment has been largely centered around the threat such a program offers to local and state control of schools. The dangers inherent in a wholesale national revision and possible attempts at standardization of curricular content, as well as, the fears that teachers will teach for assessment tests, as if they are the be all and end all of instruction, have been loudly voiced by the opponents of assessment. The proponents have countered with, in addition to statements of urgent and critical need, assurances that the diversity of our schools will be valued and maintained. Also, that any assessment plans will provide sufficient built-in safeguards designed to protect and encourage uniqueness in students and citizens. And so, in an atmosphere of uncertainity as to procedures and outcomes, of charge and counter charge, and with the very slimmest of professional majorities, we move forward into the new era of national assessment. In doing so, we are mindful that our schools have not been totally without some evaluatory experiences which should relate well to this undertaking. Most of these experiences, however, have been limited to our secondary schools.

The evaluation of high schools was begun by the state universities in the Midwest during the latter part of the nineteenth century. The purpose was two-fold: to encourage improvement in the high schools and to enable graduates of accredited high schools to enter the universities without sitting for the qualifying entrance examinations. Between the period 1910 through 1930, the high school accreditation function was transferred from the universities to state departments of education. Except for sporadic efforts by a few states to operate an accreditation-evaluation plan for elementary schools on a twelve-grade basis, accreditation by the state agencies has focused largely, if not exclusively upon the secondary school. Regional Accreditation Associations came into being after 1895, and have continued to concentrate their attention on colleges and high schools. Patrons, school boards and superintendents have worked hard to get and keep their high schools on the regional association's accredited list. However, elementary schools have been permitted to evolve as though their programs bear little or no relationship to the development of quality high schools. All too often, elementary school facilities, staffing and curriculum have suffered shameful neglect. Yet, common sense, if nothing else, tells us that a community cannot have an outstanding high school unless its organization is supported and sustained by a sound, strong and healthy elementary program.

We are embarking upon an era when systematic comprehensive evaluation is being accepted, however reluctantly, as the most promising and important tool for the maintenance and development of America's schools. At a time when federal, state and local monies are being committed as never before in a race to keep pace with societal demands, we cannot afford to ignore the obvious need for more and better educational evaluation. This need is especially acute at the much overlooked elementary level. Some organized approach must be undertaken to insure that the funds being directed toward our elementary schools are sufficient—within communities and across the nation at large. Further, these funds must be deployed to strengthen weak areas on some priority basis. A comprehensive elementary school evaluation offers the only way to determine this order of need with some measure of rationality.

ORIGINS AND EVOLUTION OF SCHOOL ASSESSMENT

All of us are aware that some colleges are quite vocal about the lack of preparation apparent in incoming freshmen classes. The high schools are performing assigned tasks in an improper and unproductive manner. Secondary school personnel denounce the lack of basic skills and concepts possessed by their students. The elementary schools are failing to function viably. While such statements may not represent the whole truth, the incidence of truth may well be present to an uncomfortably and unpardonably high degree. Strangely, the higher levels of our educational system continue to pass the fault and responsibility for student unpreparedness down. Unfortunately, its resting place, the elementary school, has traditionally been without the kind of assessment machinery available to the secondary schools and colleges. Before we examine the whys and wherefores of assessment, it should prove helpful to briefly review the origin and development of school evaluation in America.

Historically, in most nations, the task of maintaining acceptable standards in secondary schools has rested with the central government and its local agencies and sub-divisions. However, in the United States, the responsibility for secondary school appraisal has been shared among: (1) state departments of education, (2) regional accrediting associations of colleges and secondary schools, and, (3) colleges and universities. The federal government, by constitutional design, has refrained from playing a commanding role in the structuring of the accreditation and other evaluation arrangements existent to this time.

THE ROLE OF THE STATES

The constitution of every state makes some reference to education. Such references generally mandate that the legislature create and maintain a public school system. Few restrictions are placed upon the right of the legislature to control education. State departments of education serve to propose new controlling legislation and to enforce the existing statutes enacted by the legislature. In the discharge of these obligations, state departments of education exercise considerable power over both the quality and quantity of education. State legislatures, acting through state departments of education, play a major role in directing and controlling the shape and form of school systems and their instructional programs.

State departments and legislatures frequently employ one or more of the following methods in effectuating the regulation of schools:

1. Authorize local communities to engage in some educational endeavor
2. Employ state education department personnel to promote an educational cause or activity
3. Offer a non-monetary benefit for engaging in state endorsed activities
4. Furnish added state aid for local districts which cooperate in certain recommended undertakings
5. Mandate compliance by statute or state board of education rule
6. Withhold state aid because of non-compliance

Likewise, states have sought to direct the nature and scope of elementary and secondary schools by enacting specific requirements in several or all of the following areas:

1. Prescribe the minimum length of the school term
2. Set the ages of compulsory school attendance
3. Require that certain basic (common branch) and non-basic subjects be taught
4. Establish standards for teacher certification
5. Impose limits upon local borrowing and taxing powers
6. Mandate minimum salaries for instructional staff
7. Control level of state financial support
8. Dictate programs and classification procedures for handicapped children
9. Institute requirements for guidance and health services
10. Provide for statewide adoption of textbooks and supplementary teaching materials
11. Exercise approval of buildings including review of plans for all new facilities
12. Regulate matters dealing with the transportation of pupils

The above listing is certainly not intended to be an exhaustive treatment of the subject. Individual states operate in numerous additional ways to control, direct and improve education. Of one thing we can be certain. In the exercise of the rights and privileges granted by the legislatures, state departments of education are becoming steadily and increasingly involved in the establishment of more (and hopefully better) standards for elementary, as well as, secondary education.

THE EMERGENCE OF REGIONAL ACCREDITATION ASSOCIATIONS

The University of Michigan developed the first accreditation plan for secondary schools in 1872. It was designed to serve primarily as a basis for determining which local high school graduates should be granted admission priority. The response of neighboring high schools to the university conceived evaluation was most encouraging and their cooperation in the enterprise was readily forthcoming. So successful was the University of Michigan plan, that one year later, the Indiana State Department of Public Instruction acted to become the first state department of education to establish statewide accreditation criteria for secondary schools. In rapid succession, other states followed Indiana's lead. However, it was not until a quarter of a century later that the regional accreditation association concept first appeared on the educational scene. In 1895, the North Central Association of Colleges and Secondary Schools came into being and in 1902, set forth the first compilation of regionally developed standards for the accreditation of secondary schools. Three more regional associations quickly evolved; the Southern Association in 1912, the Northwest Association in 1918, and the Middle States Association in 1923. The New England Association and the Western Associations are of quite recent origins.

The standards for accreditation employed by the various regional associations have, by and large, developed from the original criteria adopted by the North Central Association in 1902. Therefore, much of what is accepted today as the yardstick against which the successes and shortcomings of secondary schools are measured, is in fact not grounded in scientifically tested fact. This should not prove too disconcerting since a good deal of research now supports the contention that educational theory may very rightly have its genesis in the ongoing practices of schools.

INFLUENCE OF COLLEGES AND UNIVERSITIES

State departments of education and regional accreditation associations are not alone in setting standards for schools. Colleges and universities wield a considerable influence upon the teaching methods and curriculum content in every elementary and secondary school. The admission requirements of institutions of higher learning determine, to no small degree, the course offerings of high schools. This is especially relevant in the case of modest sized high schools. Limited enrollments in these schools prevent a wide distribution of course offerings and force selection in favor of courses which are required for college admission. In secondary schools throughout the land, the number of pupils in such subjects as foreign languages, science and mathematics, is materially increased by virtue of the entrance requirements imposed by colleges and universities. It might further be argued that institutions of higher learning establish admission standards not unrelated to societal demands. In many instances, these demands, find crystallization in the pronouncements of professional associations and the requirement statements of the various licensing and certification bureaus.

The influence of college professors upon the programs of elementary and secondary schools is expressed through a variety of avenues. College faculty write the vast majority of textbooks used in today's schools. They develop the beliefs and attitudes of teachers who are students in professional courses. In straight subject matter courses, college faculty promote the cultural and academic knowledge and interests of those who staff our public schools. Through periodical writings, in-service training programs, work on curriculum revision projects, special purpose surveys and service on school evaluation teams, college faculty clearly mold school policy and practice.

Professors, together with state departments of education and regional accreditation associations, have been principal contributors to the evaluation and quality control standards which we find operating today. Their achievements are significant indeed, but much remains that is both unfinished and unexplored.

ELEMENTARY EVALUATION: AN ESSENTIAL CHALLENGE

Systematic elementary school evaluation offers individual schools and school systems exciting opportunities to reorder priorities, raise instructional standards, strengthen budgetary support and increase community esteem. The ways by which these much sought after and highly desirable goals might be realized unfold in preceding chapters. Suffice it to say that change at the elementary level has, until now, largely been the product of responses made to isolated crisis situations. Pressure has come from lay groups, professional associations and individuals, representing local, state and national interests. The National Defense Education Act (NDEA), for example, recently poured forth funds to upgrade elementary science and mathematics programs, and in so doing, gave national acknowledgment to the belief that these areas were in serious need of improvement. Fears associated with early Russian space explorations gave rise to this massive federally supported and sponsored program.

On the local scene, parents, board of education members and others, press sporadically for newer textbooks, better classroom lighting, greater time allotments for teaching spelling, handwriting, U.S. history, and a host of other favored subjects. Without apparent rhyme or reason, curriculum workers, principals and teachers respond to such pressure. Unsupported opinions frequently furnish the only basis for curricular action. Innovations introduced in nearby communities prompt many administrators to initiate similar changes in their own district or suffer the risk of being left far behind. And so, not as a direct result of the findings and recommendations of a systematic evaluation effort, but rather, as an emotional response to piecemeal pressures, do modifications come to our elementary schools.

Financial and personnel resources are being committed without benefit of a total appraisal. Until elementary school evaluation becomes an accepted guide for the logical ordering of priorities, there will continue to be insufficient funds directed toward elementary schools. Waste and misdirection of monies currently allotted will create a further lowering of community esteem and confidence in elementary education. The evaluation work carried on by state departments of education and colleges merits our wholehearted support and unstinting cooperation. However, the efforts of state and college must not be viewed as sufficient to satisfy all the local needs of each unique community. Schools must accept responsibility for self-evaluation. Failing this essential challenge, we must prepare ourselves to live with, and accept, the consequences of our inaction.

MOVEMENT TOWARD NATIONAL ASSESSMENT

National assessment of educational performance is presently one of the most hotly debated and potentially important issues in American education. No one appears to question the fact that we fall woefully short of the essential information required to carry out our stated educational purposes and goals. Number of facts memorized, degree of ability to reason and admission rate to college, are some of the isolated and diverse statistics currently employed to measure the success of schools in educating children and youth. Some universally acceptable standards must be established to assess educational output. Thus far, educators engaged in the national assessment debate have, for the most part, become embroiled not in the true need for assessment but rather in the dangers and evils of "testing" and "test result comparisons."

Assessment should not singularly imply universal national testing. The sciences of statistical sampling and computerization have advanced to the point where answers accurate within five percent can be achieved even from a very limited number of sampled cases. The pressing need for national assessment has already been clearly established and set forth. Now, theory and technology have developed to the point where assessment on a national scale can become a reality.

Large and strong professional groups including: the National Education Association, American Association of School Administrators, National Secondary School Principals Association, and the National Elementary School Principals Association have, after agonizing debate, gone on record as favoring a national assessment program. However, their position of support is not without some important qualification. These groups insist that any national program of educational assessment be conducted by an agency which is not only objective, credible to the public and competent, but also is quasi-legal and therefore possessing a degree of public accountability. Further, they demand that any assessment undertaken promote differences in educational goals, programs and structures that correspond to and are compatable with the educational needs and assets of different geographical regions, different school districts and different students. The aforementioned organizations are resolute in their determination to strongly oppose any attempt to implement national testing or a national curriculum that seeks to measure all districts and students by a single standard. The concept of different standards or programs suited to local educational situations must prevail, or lacking the necessary support of the powerful educational associations which espouse this viewpoint, any national assessment attempt is doomed to failure.

ESTABLISHMENT OF THE ASSESSMENT AGENCY

With the agreement of forty states, two U.S. territories and the U.S. Office of Education, a quasi-legal organization, the Education Commission of the States, was established and in mid-1969, assumed full governance of America's first national school assessment project. The Commission was funded for 1969 at $2.5 million: the 1970 budget of $4 million was provided by the U.S. Office of Education and major private foundations. The initial goal of ECS was to design and carry out a project consisting of the nationwide assessment of 9, 13, and 17 year olds in the areas of citizenship, science and writing. Within six months after accepting responsibility for the assessment project, the Education Commission of the States announced that the immediate and long range schedule of their National Assessment of Educational Progress Project had been broadened and rearranged as follows:

Cycle 1

March 1969-February 1970 Science, Writing, Citizenship
October 1970-August 1971 Reading, Literature
October 1971-August 1971 Music, Social Studies
October 1971-August 1973 Math, Science, Career and Occupational Development
October 1973-August 1974 Reading, Writing, Listening and Speaking
October 1974-August 1975 Citizenship, Art, Consumer Education

Cycle 2

1975-76 Math, Science, Health Education
1976-77 Reading, Literature, Physical Education
1977-78 Music, Social Studies, Study Skills
1978-79 Math, Science, Career and Occupational Development
1979-80 Reading, Writing, Listening and Speaking
1980-81 Citizenship, Art, Consumer Education

It is the expressed intention of ECS to reassess the basic subjects—reading, mathematics and science—in a three year cycle. The assessment policy committee (ECS) explains that the three-year cycle will permit comparisons to determine what changes have taken place. Assessment will be made in four regions: north, south, central and west; in urban centers, small towns and rural areas; by economic levels, sex and race. The instruments thus far employed are especially designed for ECS by leading test makers. They are not a substitute for present national standardized tests.

The expansion and intensification of the testing calendar, as shown above, should not be interpreted as a signification of a philosophical encroachment upon the originally agreed upon aims, purposes and values of national assessment. If anything, it appears to be a more genuine and realistic expression of the desperate need to measure educational effectiveness on a broad enough front so as to establish priorities within the whole of the curricular pattern.

The July 1969, issue of, "The School Administrator," a monthly publication of the American Association of School Administrators, announced that the main purpose of the Education Commission of the States' assessment project is to ". . . measure the educational return on the dollars invested."[1] No other purposes, main or secondary, were set forth. Those who have fought the hard fight for national assessment most assuredly know that a measurement of dollar value is an expected and welcome outcome, but certainly such an aim can not be considered by thoughtful citizens and educators as the sole purpose of assessment. Encouragingly, in subsequent publications the AASA offers more than ample evidence that it does not truly subscribe to such a restrictive statement of assessment purpose. Indeed, the position papers of all the major professional associations speak as one in emphasizing that a far more important and fundamental purpose of national assessment is the measurement of how well the schools of America are preparing their students for productive, stable and satisfying adult lives—the measurement of dollar value is an important by-product of the assessment activity.

THE LIKELIHOOD OF ELEMENTARY SCHOOL ACCREDITATION

The establishment of a national assessment program which includes elementary age youngsters; the accelerated planning activity of state departments of education in the field of elementary school evaluation; and, the increased voluntary use of the self-evaluation process by individual schools and school districts, lends support to the contention that elementary school accreditation will be a next logical step in the evolutionary sequence. In each of the aforementioned evaluative approaches limitations are readily apparent. The national assessment effort is totally concerned with the measurement of what pupils have learned. Instructional facilities, staff qualifications, teaching techniques, among other things, are not assessed. The evaluation plans of state departments are still largely directed toward the measurement of items which serve to determine the basis for distribution of state aid. The amount of expenditures per pupil, the square footage requirement for classrooms, the adequacy of playground areas, enrollment limitations in kindergarten classes and a host of other facts essential to arriving at an equable state aid formula, create the main point of emphasis in evaluations conducted by state departments of education. It is doubtful that this emphasis will ever be otherwise. More and more educators express the belief that state departments of education, saddled with financial and legislative accountability, are not likely to develop and foster objective evaluation proposals which encourage innovation and individuality within the schools. Self-evaluation of elementary schools, either with or without a visiting team, undoubtedly offers the best opportunity for total review and appraisal yet devised. The locally determined evaluation instrument can include criteria selected from the widest possible range of choice. Staff and community involvement can be sustained and directed toward a high level of productive yield. Through such an effort, the needs of the unique student body served can best be met. We should, however, hasten to add that the voluntary self-evaluation of elementary schools does not carry with it the same pressure for corrective actions that failure to achieve regional accreditation brings to secondary schools.

---

[1] American Association of School Administrators, "Hazlett Directs Assessment for ECS." *The School Administrator,* Washington, D.C.: The Association, July, 1969, p. 12.

Until the full weight of a K-12 grade regional accreditation plan can be introduced, many weaknesses and shortcomings found to exist at the elementary level will go uncorrected. This prospect, however, should not serve to detract from the wholesome atmosphere for improvement which is engendered by the initiation of a self-evaluation study. Inclusion of the elementary schools in a total K-12 grade regional accreditation plan seems inevitable, but until that date arrives, self-evaluation offers the best opportunity for improving and strengthening programs at the elementary level.

Index

197

Q

R